DYING:
AN INTRODUCTION

DYING:
AN INTRODUCTION

Poems by

L. E. SISSMAN

An Atlantic Monthly Press Book
LITTLE, BROWN AND COMPANY · BOSTON · TORONTO

LIBRARY OF CONGRESS CATALOG CARD NO. 67-23837

FIRST EDITION

The author wishes to thank the following publications, in which many of the poems appeared, for their kind permission to reprint them here: *The Atlantic, Boston, The Harvard Alumni Bulletin, The New Yorker,* and *The Review* of Oxford University, England.

Poems that first appeared in *The New Yorker* are "Going Home, 1945," "Henley, July 4: 1914–1964," "A College Room: Lowell R-54, 1945," "The Birdman of Cambridge, Mass.," "Stillman Infirmary," "New England: Dead of Winter," "In and Out," "Two Encounters," "A Day in the City," "Sweeney to Mrs. Porter in the Spring," "On the Island," "Two Happenings in Boston," "The West Forties: Morning, Noon, and Night," and "Dying: An Introduction."

ATLANTIC–LITTLE, BROWN BOOKS
ARE PUBLISHED BY
LITTLE, BROWN AND COMPANY
IN ASSOCIATION WITH
THE ATLANTIC MONTHLY PRESS

*Published simultaneously in Canada
by Little, Brown & Company (Canada) Limited*

PRINTED IN THE UNITED STATES OF AMERICA

for
Anne

Thanks

to E. A. Muir, Howard Moss, Peter Davison, Will
Davenport, Jerrold Hickey, Dorothy Burnham Eaton,
and my parents for help of many kinds in bringing these
poems to print.

Though you acquire
The best attire,
Appearing fine and fair,
Yet death will come
Into the room,
And strip you naked there.

—"An Address to All Concerning Death"
American, anonymous, nineteenth century

Contents

IV

V

VI

VII

One

I

Going Home, 1945

Home is so sad. It stays as it was left . . .
—*Philip Larkin*

I. GETTING THERE

1. Night

"En route aboard the Twentieth Century
Limited," says the club-car notepaper.
With a glad cry, I take a seat and write
Six crested notes to six deserving friends
Who need a lesson in my eminence,
Or on whose female persons I have vain
Designs. Speaking of female persons, who
Is that old-fashioned girl three seats away,
With maraschino-cherry lips and teeth
As white as lemon pith, with ice-blue eyes
And amber Bourbon hair? Must be Bryn Mawr.
Above my station, which is G.C.T.,
And, at the other end, Fort Street. I cock
An innocent index at the bar waiter,
And call, in a bass tenor, for a Scotch
And branch water. (I hope that branch water
Is carried on crack trains. I think of it
In pear-shaped bottles, like Perrier.) The black
White-coated waiter makes ironically
Over my disarray. "Mix, sir?" "Uh-huh,"
I grunt. Branch water gets no rise,
Not even one eyelid bat, from Bryn Mawr.
I give up and tack back to my roomette,
Where Webster waits to take me by the throat
And threaten me to sleep. "Or with his nails

He'll dig them up again." Amen. I doze,
Until, in the marshalling yards of Buffalo,
The nails of couplings dig me up again.
Up the trick curtain; under it, the moon
Face of the station clock beams a huge One
Into my dilatory pupil. Sleep
Returns for his lost westbound passenger
And hustles him aboard. They couple up
Another Hudson 4-6-4 and I awake
Again. The clock says two. We're off. Good night.

2. Dawn

Morning is not a matter of whiskbroom
Paradiddles on sack-suit shoulders; not
A throb of chocolate voices in the men's
Washroom; not an aubade of good cigars
Smoking on sink rims while their masters shave
In undershirts, pending suspenders; not
Steam rising from the ranks of sinks where jokes
Go off so limply at this hour — "Mister,
Your sign fell down!" (Laughter) — and one man drinks
Rye by himself in a toilet stall; morning is not
That any more at all, but a shave alone
In my roomette and a walk to the dining car,
And breakfast in silence on the Century.

3. Noon

Nous sommes arrivés. The old Lafayette
Coach which my dad affects awaits without,
While my dim mother pins me in a grip
Of flesh and blood. Just two semesters stand
Between me and these twin authorities,
The moon and sun, ruling me night and day
In opposition and conjunction. Now

I stoop to inspect their tiny orrery,
Worked by a crank from higher up, a god
From the Machine-Design Department. We
Climb in the fatal car and head for home
Through widened streets lined with diminished shops,
Patrolled by shrivelled people, shrunken kids,
And miniature dogs. Waste paper blows
For miles along the thoroughfares toward
The straightedge of the horizon, where the world,
Seeing me entering my father's house,
Awaits my resurrection in the fall.

II. AT HOME

1. The Room

The next of kin is marched into a dark,
North-oriented room where trumpet vines
And overhanging eaves restrain the light,
There to confront the body of his past:
A matter of identity. Look, those
Are spectacles that were his eyes. That book
Was his vocabulary. That wall map
(Out of the *Geographic*) was his world.
That copy of "Jane's Fighting Ships" was all
His insular defense. Those model planes —
Stormovik, Stuka, ME-109 —
Were his air arm, which tirelessly traversed
The compass rose around its dusty strings.
Who was this recent tenant of my room?
Intelligence demands an answer. "Why,
I never saw the boy before in my life."

2. The Folks

My father casts a stone whose ripples ride
Almost to my unhearing aid, the ear.

My answering fire likewise falls short. Between
Us lies no-generation's land, a waste
Of time. Barbed wire and trenches separate
The conscript class of 1895
From that of 1928. I see
My father, in a tall examination room
Gaslit by fishtail burners, demonstrate
The differential calculus; he sees
Me boozing with low types in Central Square
And touching tasty women on the quick.
(Not such a bad idea, Dad, after all.)
Had he his way, his little mathemat
Would be devouring sums and public praise
Like any Univac; and had I mine,
My dad and I would be out on the town,
Like as a brother act in our black ties,
Clubbable, bibulous, sly, debonair.
Fat chance of that. Across the timing gap
No blue spark fires. We talk in circles which
Are not contiguous. It is too bad
Our purposes for others founder on
Their purposes for us. Now, take my dad.

3. The Date

Hat holds me at an angle to survey
My metamorphosis from local boy
To Eastern College Man. Light years away,
Her once and future beaux from Tech and State
Back, blinded, into corners of the room,
Bedazzled by my meteoric rise.
All night, respectfully, their voices flat
As the land's lie, they ask me what it's like
Back there, incredulously fingering
My J. Press jacket, softly crying "Cool!"

Like pigeons. And the girls! Such nattering —
Which even bird conventions cannot touch —
Alarms my keeper, Hat, to vigilance
Over her showpiece, lest I taste too much
Of all I'm offered. But it doesn't matter;
The *pièce de résistance* is Harriet later.

4. The Chum

It's Harvard vs. Williams at the D.-
A.C. Out of my corner armchair, I
Dance nimbly to clasp hands with Richie B.
Mackenzie, my old challenger. Now he,
The shorter fighter, boards his bicycle,
And pedals up to me. Right cross; we shake,
Break clean. On to the greater battle, where
The muffled musketry of cutlery
Rattles a rapid fire above the dull
Trench-mortar thuds of crockery. "A dry
One with a twist." "Bourbon and branch water."
"Blue points." "Cracked crab." "The grayling amandine."
"Filet mignon. Pommes allumettes." "Roquefort."
"Blue cheese." "Rosé?" "Rosé." "There's no place like —"
"Cambridge. Boy, what a wild —" "Woman I met
At Bennington." "I'll tell the world they put
Out. Why —" "They don't pass out, I'll never know."
"Two great big townies —" "Landed on their ear
Outside the bar. From Rensselaer." "No kid?"
"I swear." "Rum cake." "Profiteroles."
"Cointreau." "Martell." "Gentlemen's grades. Three 'C's,
A 'D'." "Still worse — two 'D's. On pro." "No kid?"
"I'll pay." "Let me." "I'll pay." "Let me." "O.K."
The winner and still champion is me.

5. *The Town*

In this al fresco gallery of Sheelers —
Replete with stacks and tipples, ramps and hoppers,
Vents, derricks, ducts, louvers, and intercoolers —
I wander lonely as a cloud. Here is the beauty
Of this ridiculous, gas-smelling city.
Not those gilt towers stuck up so proudly
To spell a skyline, not those too loudly
Dulcet and unobtrusively huge houses
Dotting the northern suburbs. No, the heart
Of it is where its masters' love is:
In the cold-rolling mills, annealing rooms,
Pickling and plating vats, blast furnaces,
Drop-forging shops, final-assembly lines:
Wherever angular, ideal machines,
Formed seamlessly of unalloyed desire,
Strike worthless stereotypes out of the fire.

6. *The Room, 8/31*

Lieutenant Kije, for the twentieth time
On record, tramps the dogged August night
In glacé top boots, jangling all his high
Orders of Irony and Satire. My
Suffering mother passes through the wall
A muffled *cri de coeur:* "Turn that thing down,"
To which I courteously defer. The summer stands
Suspended in its bowl, and also runs
At a great rate down the drain somehow, dragging
Me into fall. There still remain these nights
Of close restraint in heat, a camisole
Of dampness wired for the amazingly
Loud sound of streetcars roller-skating; for

The shocking sight of their electric-blue
Stars overhead; for their galvanic smell
Of ozone; and the unforgettable scent
Of air-conditioned drugstores, where the pure
Acid of citrus cuts across the fat
Riches of chocolate, subjugates perfume
(Evening in Paris), soap, iodoform.
Back in my heated room with the night game
And Nine Elizabethan Dramatists,
I chill myself with Webster. In the twelfth,
August strikes out and thunders to the showers.

III. AWAY

1. Packing

Admit the sophomore's impediments
In the Caesarean sense: the stuff I lug
Wisely and foolishly out of the breach
In mother's privet hedge, in father's picket fence.
Item: one pair of officer's pink pants
Left over from R.O.T.C.; one tam
Worn by the Pictou Highlanders and me;
One six-foot Princeton scarf; one pair sweatpants;
Two white bucks aged to grey; one copy each
Of "Dubliners," "Wind in the Willows," "Kim,"
"Tropic of Cancer," "House at Pooh Corner," "Teen-
Age Etiquette," "Ulysses," "Leaves of Grass,"
"A Child's Garden of Verses," "Four Quartets,"
"Tarr," "Peter Rabbit," "Lady Chatterley";
One Remington Electric Shaver; six
Giant Almond Hershey Bars; one roll of Tums;
One jar of Mum; one tube of Pepsodent;
One guest bar of Camay; two Trojans; three
Packs of Balkan Sobranie cigarettes;
A secret diary (three entries), and

A tangled mass too numerous to list.
I genuflect on the stuffed leatherette
Until the straining snap locks creak and catch;
Then I pick up my bags, one in each hand,
And take the first step to Jerusalem,
New England's green and pleasant land.

2. Parting

"Caoutchouc," I comment, flexing my big feet
In their new gum-boots. "Are you catching cold?"
Mother demands. "Uh, no. Just practicing
A new word." "Good. Do you have everything?"
"Uh, yes. Umbrella, earmuffs, undershirts —"
"The marmalade!" "Oh, hell!" "Your grandmother
Will just be sick. She got it from Dundee."
"Ship it." "It's glass. I can't." "Here comes the train.
Son, have a good year," my poor father says.
His eyes belie his smile. But he's a good,
Though steady, loser. Now, fraternally,
He takes my hand in the firm, funny grip
Of the Order of Fathers and Sons. My mother plants
A moist and plosive kiss across my ear,
Mumbles, and sheds a shiny patent tear.

3. Starting

Gathering way, we step out of the station
Gingerly, silver showing at the forefoot
Of the long engine, and a curl of cream
Whipped at her whistle. How superior
It is to pass clean through the roots of each
Bystander's real life and leave the city
In the lurch like a wife. My guilt is packed
In with my sweatshirts in the baggage car;

I travel light. Brick tenements sprint by,
All up to here with melodrama, kids,
Mice, misery. I blink and miss a block,
Yawn and omit a mile. Now the Toltec
Pyramids of plants appear and pivot by.
Soon rolling mills give way to fields of rye.
It's reading period: "Wish me good speed;
For I am going into a wilderness."
The sun goes west; the sky goes black; it is
Full tide 'tween night and day. Just in the nick,
Bosola, in a mist, I know not how,
Receives his mortal wound at cocktail time.
I home in on the club car, straightening
The rucked-up jacket I've been reading in,
And take a seat with *Fortune* on my knee.
The waiter fetches Scotch and branch water.
Say, who's that Highland tycoon's fetching daughter
In a dress-Stewart skirt, with Shetland hair,
Eyes like a loch, breasts like a ben? She's mine,
Assuming I can take a dare. With luck,
From now until tomorrow is today,
From here over the hills and far away,
We'll kiss and play and possibly make free,
En route aboard the Twentieth Century.

Parents in Winter

I. MOTHER AT THE PALACE, 1914

In ragtime, when my mother ran away
From flat Ontario with Art to play
A fair Ophelia on the two-a-day
Time of that time, she was just seventeen
And far behind her figure and her face
In bearing, aim, and point: one more good kid
To swell a progress or to farce a scene
With slim impersonations of a race
Of royal losers, which is what she did.

Until, until. Until, in Buffalo,
The Rep played out its string and let her go,
And she tried out before the morning show
By gaslight in the cold Academy
For right end in the chorus, which required
An elemental sense of rhythm, and
A dauntless liking for variety,
And a good pair of legs, which she had. Hired,
She danced split weeks across the level land.

In Dayton, at the little Lyceum,
She was first billed with Andy as a team —
Shannon & Anderson — a waking dream
Worth thirty dollars weekly. Soon, in Troy,
Her act was spotted by Gus McAdoo,
Who made her both a single and a star
At twenty; and, in the blood-tasting joy
Of early triumph, barely twenty-two,
She played the Palace just before the war.

The times forbid me to imagine all
The grandnesses of that high music hall
Upon her opening, when, at her call,
Packards and Pierces inlaid new-laid snow
With their non-skid tread, largely loitering
While their Van Bibber owners drank her in
Through two-power pearl Zeiss glasses, in a glow
Of carbon-arc limelight wherein she sang,
En Dutch girl, to those white fronts that were men,

"When I wore a tulip." Many a rose
Made its red way toward her ravished nose
With its eleven peers and one of those
White cards of invitation and entrée
To a man's world of idleness and grace,
Leather and liquor and less fluent night
Exchanges than one would expect, and day
After day embowered alone to face
Oneself returning singly from the night.

"You great big beautiful doll," she sang, but "No,"
She said to her appraisers, who would go
To any lengths for her after the show.
I wonder why she did. Perhaps she saw
No commonness in their inheritance
And her upstart career; perhaps she felt
The condescension in their bids, their law
Of put and call. Instead, she chose to dance
And sing on in the hand that chance had dealt.

I wonder, too: was it her Irish pride
That made her tell the man she would not ride,
And so turn down a rôle with Bonafide
Films, Limited, and so turn down a road

That was to lead to giving up the stage
And taking up the piano, to her glory,
And winning the Bach prize, and having sowed
Such seeds and oats, at last to marriage,
And so to me? But that's another story.

II. FATHER AT PACKARD'S, 1915

The brick plant like a school. The winter set
Of East Grand Boulevard. The violets
Of dawn relent to let us see the first
Shift of its students hurrying to class
Distinction in the undistinguished mass
Concealing offices and cubicles,
Great drawing rooms with draftsmen on their stools,
Foremen's rude cabins bringing outdoors in,
Craftsmen's workbenches littered with their trim
Brushes and colors, and, in Main, the lines
Of workers in their hundreds vanishing,
With our perspective, at the end of all
The crucial stations in their longsome hall.
Here comes my father. Look how thin he is.
See snowflakes flower on the blank plat of his
Forehead. Note his black hair. In hand,
He has already all the instruments
(Pre-war and German in their provenance)
To tap and die a life. Intolerant
To the last thousandth, they encompass all
Protracted elevations of his soul,
And in their narrow ink lines circumscribe
The isometric renderings of pride
Which will propel him through the glacial years
While he designs the sun and planet gears.

East Congress and McDougall Streets, Detroit, May 25

Now winter leaves off worrying our old slum,
And summer comes.
Already docks,
Daisies and dandelions, thistles and hollyhocks
Begin to camouflage the tin in vacant lots.
(Some vegetable god ordains these plots
Of plants to rule the earth.
Their green clothes mask the birth-
Marks of a blight.)
Look down the street: there is nobody in sight
As far as Mount Elliott Avenue (where
We kids in knickers took a double dare
To hop a Grand Trunk freight;
Where, every night,
Those marvellous whistles came from).
This dead kingdom,
Composed of empty shanties under the sun,
The arc lamp swinging overhead (the one
That hung there in 1930), the same sidewalks
Of dog-eared squares of slate marked with the chalks
Of the persisting children, the sad board
Fences which shored
Up private property falling into the alley,
This was Jerusalem, our vivid valley.

In our dead neighborhood
Now nothing more can come to any good.

Least of all the Victorian orphanage that still stands
Behind an ironic fence on its own grounds
Diagonally opposite.
The convict children have forsaken it:
In one mad prison break, foiling their guards,
They burst out from its wards —
Long as the Hall of Mirrors, high as a kite,
Carved like a cuckoo clock, capped with grey slate —
Leaving an archive of curses on its walls,
A dado of dirt at hand height in its halls,
And a declivity in each doorsill.
Now the street-Arabian artillery
Has lobbed a brick into each gallery
And opened every window from afar.
Each outer door, ajar,
Is a safe conduct to the rat,
The mouse, the alley cat.
Under its exaggerated eaves,
The orphanage endures. Here nothing leaves,
Nothing arrives except ailanthus trees.

My thirst for the past is easy to appease.

II

Henley, July 4: 1914-1964

Fifty years after Capt. Leverett Saltonstall's Harvard junior
varsity became the first American eight to win the Grand Chal-
lenge Cup at Henley in England, Saltonstall . . . will lead his
crew back to the scene of its triumph. Every man who pulled
an oar in the victorious 1914 Harvard crew, as well as the
coxswain, is not only alive but is preparing to return to Henley
on July 1. They will take to a shell again on the picturesque
Thames course during the forthcoming regatta.

— *The New York Times*

Fair stands the wind again
For nine brave Harvard men
Sung by both tongue and pen,
    Sailing for Henley
Fifty years after they
Won the great rowing fray
On Independence Day,
    Boyish and manly.

On Independence Day
Fifty light years away
They took the victor's bay
    From mighty Britain.
They were a City joke
Till they put up the stroke
And their strong foemen broke,
    As it is written.

Leverett Saltonstall
Is the first name of all
That noble roll we call,
    That band of brothers.
Curtis, Talcott, and Meyer,

Morgan and Lund set fire
To England's funeral pyre,
    They and three others.

That young and puissant crew
Quickened their beat and flew
Past all opponents, who
    Watched them in wonder.
Fifty years later, we
See them across the sea
Echo that memory
    Like summer thunder.

Fair stands the wind again;
Thames, bear them softly, then.
Far came these rowing men
    In every weather.
What though their stroke has slowed?
(How long they all have rowed!)
Oarsmen, accept our ode,
    Blades of a feather.

A College Room: Lowell R-34, 1945

A single bed. A single room. I sing
Of man alone on the skew surface of life.
No kith, no kin, no cat, no kid, no wife,
No Frigidaire, no furniture, no ring.

Yes, but the perfect state of weightlessness
Is a vacuum the natural mind abhors:
The strait bed straightway magnetizes whores;
The bare room, aching, itches to possess.

Thus I no sooner shut the tan tin door
Behind me than I am at once at home.
Will I, nill I, a budget pleasure dome
Will rear itself in Suite R-34.

A pleasure dome of Klees and Watteaus made,
Of chairs and couches from the Fair Exchange,
Of leavings from the previous rich and strange
Tenant, of fabrics guaranteed to fade.

Here I will entertain the young idea
Of Cambridge, wounded, winsome, and sardonic;
Here I will walk the uttermost euphonic
Marches of English, where no lines are clear.

Here I will take the interchangeable
Parts of ephemerid girls to fit my bed;
Here death will first enter my freshman head
On a visitor's passport, putting one tangible

Word in my mouth, a capsule for the day
When I will be evicted from my home
Suite home so full of life and damned to roam
Bodiless and without a thing to say.

FOOTNOTE: MRS. CIRCASSIAN

An orphan home. But into this eclectic
Mass of disasters sails Mrs. Circassian,
Maid without parallel, queen beyond question
Of household gods, gas and electric.

She puts the room right with a basilisk
Look, pats it into shape like a pillow;
Under her hard hand, the Chinese willow
Learns how to live with an abstraction. Risk

All and win all is her maiden motto,
Which makes mere matter fall into its place,
Dress right and form platoons to save its face,
And suffers Pollock to lie down with Watteau.

The Birdman of Cambridge, Mass.

How odd, in his odd trousers and odd coat,
Herron appears to strangers in his field.
Standing stock-straight in brown, he may not yield
Even his presence to intruders. Note,

However, the harsh characteristic cry
He often utters to his kind; his old
And drafty house, forever damp and cold;
His grey legs, Shetland jacket, and light tie.

All fine field marks, but nothing to his grin,
Bent and concealing a long rusty laugh,
His long-nosed long head stuffed with birdman's chaff —
A perfect specimen of the odd man in.

The Savage, Gore Hall G-31

(For H. B.)

The poor Near North Side Bigfoot In-di-an,
Deadeye, draws back the arc of aching steel
Another eighth of an inch. Cochineal
Glimmers and trembles just across the span,

A foot from its blank target. Now his thumb
Cranks the Nth degree of pitch onto the blade
Of the minute ballista which has laid
Siege to the Tabula Rasa since the drum

Of Bigfoot first flammed into old Newtown.
Splat. Now the missile which he has let fly
Colorfully crosses the gap, hits the bull's eye,
Dum, dum, with its soft nose, spreads and runs down.

Stand back to see what Deadeye is up to:
Attacking, in his irregular uniform
Of jeans and moccasins, the still white form
Of his opponent, shot and bleeding through

The canvas ever more copiously.
Fighting for altitude, a lumpen moon
Clears the horizon like a free balloon
With squarish corners and tacks up the sky

Which is jet black. The Indian, done, steps back,
A sight in his war paint, ultramarine
Streaks on his forehead, madder and chrome green
Spots on his cheekbones, gouts of crimson lake

In his ink hair. Perfumed by turpentine,
But white and tame again, he puts on clean
Field's clothes and claims his old seat on the machine.
Together, Deadeye and I step out to dine.

Behind us in the dark, the painted moon
Keeps rising in the artificial sky
Until at last it cannot tell a lie
And lights that landscape up as bright as noon.

Up All Night, Adams House C-55

Dead on the dot of dawn, the Orient
Express steams in the window where we sit.
Its headlight hits Henry Kerr right in the eye.
Lightened by loosing the sandbags of sleep,
We bob about C Entry's ceilings like
So many free balloons, still full of gas
From yesterday, while out in Plympton Street
The air, recharged with light, proclaims today
To its great public, and one rusty ray
Of sun, noon-bound, takes hold on Randolph Hall,
And caroms down, diluted, into all
Shades of Aurora on the brick sidewalk
Beside the charcoal street, all business —
Coal carts, milk wagons, and newspaper trucks —
At this ungodly and almighty hour.
"Kant," Henry tries to say, producing just
A peanut-whistle husk, but we all know
Which *philosophe* he means. "I don't buy Kant,"
Says Parsons. "Now, you take Descartes and see —"
"You take Descartes," I interrupt, and down
The lees of my rum Coke. "Let's all get down
And eat before it gets too jammed, and take
A walk." "All right, let's go!" Each with his green
And inky copy of the *Crimson* in
His inky hand, a badge of editors,
We march like marshals down the dusty flights
Of stony steps to the subalterns' mess,
In clouds of power and manly sleeplessness.

The Museum of Comparative Zoology

Struck dumb by love among the walruses
And whales, the off-white polar bear with stuffing
Missing, the mastodons like muddy busses,
I sniff the mothproof air and lack for nothing.

A general grant enabled the erection,
Brick upon brick, of this amazing building.
Today, in spite of natural selection,
It still survives an orphan age of gilding.

Unvarnished floors tickle the nose with dust
Sweeter than any girls' gymnasium's;
Stove polish dulls the cast-iron catwalk's rust;
The soot outside would make rival museums

Blanch to the lintels. So would the collection.
A taxidermist has gone ape. The cases
Bulging with birds whose differences defy detection
Under the dirt are legion. Master races

Of beetles lie extinguished in glass tables:
Stag, deathwatch, ox, dung, diving, darkling, May.
Over the Kelmscott lettering of their labels,
Skeleton crews of sharks mark time all day.

Mark time: these groaning boards that staged a feast
Of love for art and science, since divorced,
Still scantily support the perishing least
Bittern and all his kin. Days, do your worst:

No more of you can come between me and
This place from which I issue and which I
Grow old along with, an unpromised land
Of all unpromising things that live and die.

This brick ark packed with variant animals —
All dead — by some progressive-party member
Steams on to nowhere, all the manuals
Of its calliope untouched, toward December.

Struck dumb by love among the walruses
And whales, the off-white polar bear with stuffing
Missing, the mastodons like muddy busses,
I sniff the mothproof air and lack for nothing.

Stillman Infirmary

Clowning with you, I fell into Lake Waban
In late November and ended up in Stillman.
Was a loose kiss in the dark Agora
Worth such an earache and so much penicillin?

Why, yes. Where else was my grandmother's house
Open for business? Where else was the "in"
Sheet signed by three white shifts of nursing mothers?
Where else was food so innocent and filling?
Where else could wards make only children brothers?
Where else, if you were young and weak and willing
And suitably infected, would they ease you
Of all impediments except your childhood,
One almost insupportable snatch of river
Twisting to westward, and the smell of woodwork?

Today some civil servant must deliver
Us from all this strong languor and abolish
Our ultimate retreat, which he has done.

Passing the site, driving along the river,
I see apartments sprung up from the ashes
Of my late childhood. Farther east, the skyline
Is made and broken by a topless tower
Of wet white concrete painted by Dong Kingman.
Its name is Hygiene. Its mauve curtains shelter
New men who need not ever go to Stillman.

Clowning with you, I fell into Lake Waban.
I wonder where you currently are matron.
I wonder if you ever think of clowning.
I wonder if I could have stayed in Stillman.

New England: Dead of Winter

Whether this impulse was a "renaissance" or only
an "Indian summer," as Mr. Santayana has called it
. . . the impulse existed and the movement was real.
— *Van Wyck Brooks*

Augustin Dunster Saylor Sayward now
Undoes his side door to the likes of me,
And hands me up into his rarefied
And rubber-smelling entry, where a pride
Of marble literary lions cows
Me in the antlers of an oak coat tree,
Vetting the unlicked cub for keeping size.

Homer, whose head is twice the span of mine,
Looks down on me in spades with twice-blind eyes;
The Bard looks dirks. Professor Sayward comes
Hotfoot to claim me. His whole household hums
The high harmonics of a mighty line
He is the end of. Only empty skies
Exist past the slim volume of his smile,

Still cased in its worn pink dust cover.
We walk upstairs in the eclectic style
Of Colonel Captain Doctor Saylor, who
Came back from Lexington and Canton blue,
Wore blue again before the war was over,
And left two blueblood legs on Malvern Hill.
The study: in a cunning China trade,

The rude West was exchanged for Eastern guile,
Which, when transported and translated, made

This faded, dazzling room of overripe
Blue, gold, and amber fruit the prototype
Of all Chinesery, set off with tiles,
Italicized with a bronzed Tuscan maid,
Completed with a period Morris chair.

Above the Gothic desk, the dull-gold wall
Displays the leonine and dogged stare
Of Augustin the First, the ur, the great
Augustin Dunster Saylor, where too late
The sweet birds sang of Arthur in his hall,
God in his Heaven, Saylor in his chair
Of English Literature in Harvard Yard.

"My grandfather was great," his scion mutters.
I answer that he was indeed a bard.
(Unlike Professor S., industrious
And able critic of illustrious
American authors, save his forefathers.)
He jots an introduction on his card —
"Do show your work to dear Professor Dix"—
And bows me out to nineteen forty-six.

In and Out: Severance of Connections, 1946

1. Civis

Walking the town as if I owned it all —
Each lilac leafing out in Brattle Street,
Each green vane in the hollow square guarding
The gargoyles on Memorial Hall, each inch
Of rubber tubing in the Mallinckrodt
Chemical Laboratory, each
Particle who would learn and gladly teach,
Each English bicycle chained to its rack,
Each green bag humping on its scholar's back,
Each tally for a Cambridge traffic death,
Each boyish girl who makes you catch your breath,
Each Argyle sock, each Bursar's bill, each ounce
Of shag, each brick, each doctorate — as if
I owned the entire spring-wound town, I walk
Up the north path to University Hall.

2. Magister

The Master's teeth squeak as he sprinkles me
(Too hot to handle) with a mist of spit
That dries quite coolly. "Edwards, I've got some
Rough news for you." In his glazed, padded, blue
Old double-breasted serge suit and his bat-
Wing bow tie (navy, with pink polka dots),
He lets me have it right between the eyes,
His aces on the table, man to boy.
"Look, if there's one thing I can't tolerate

It's smart guys that won't work. The deans are soft
On geniuses. Not me. What we need more
Of is Midwestern athletes who get C's."
He stands up to reveal that his brown vest
Is perfectly misbuttoned. "Now, don't think
That I'm the least bit sorry about you.
I'm sorry for your mother and your dad.
You let them down. Now, you get out of here
And do something worthwhile. Work with your hands.
Stick with it two years. Maybe they'll take you back.
Okay, fella? That's it. Now let's shake."
We shake. I shake in secret with the shame of it.

3. *Exilium*

The ghost goes south, avoiding well-worn ways
Frequented by his friends. Instead, he slips
Into loose shadows on the sunless side
Of the least-travelled street. But even there,
One with a bony finger points him out
And pierces him with questions. Zigzagging,
He hedges hastily back to his route,
Which leads on past his windows, tendrilly
Embraced already by the outriders
Of summer's ivy, past his pipes and books
And dirty shirts and mother's picture, past
The dining hall where his name is still good
For a square meal, no questions asked, and past
The common room which is too good for him.
Across the Drive his beast heaves into view:
A monster boathouse lolling on the bank
Of the high river, backside in the water.
Inside, he greets the landlord's black-haired daughter,
Miss Jacobs, with a nod, and goes upstairs

To put his chamois-seated crew pants on.
Then, past the ranks of Compromises, he
Walks out to the land's end of the long float,
Selects his Single, and stands out to sea.

III

In and Out: A Home Away from Home, 1947

1. *One O'Clock*

With gin, *prosciutto,* and Drake's Devil Dogs
In a brown-paper bag, I climb the Hill
On Saturday, the thirty-first of May,
Struck by the sun approaching apogee,
Green comments issued by the Common trees,
Mauve decadence among magnolias,
The moving charcoal shadows on the brown
Stone of the moving brownstone where I live,
And a spring breath of Lux across the Charles.
My key mutters the password; I step in
To the dense essence of an entire past:
Rugs, chicken, toilets, Lysol, dust, cigars.
Through that invisible nerve gas (which leads
In time to total incapacity),
I climb the two flights to my little flat.

2. *Two-Thirty*

Done with the Devil Dogs, I take the brush
Out of the tooth glass and decant my first
Gin of the afternoon. In half an hour
She will be here. All is in readiness:
The bedspread taut, the ashtrays wiped, a glass
Swiped from the bathroom down the hall, a small
Plate of *prosciutto* canapés. Now Fu
Manchu reclines at ease in his hideaway,
While his nets, broadcast, sweep their victim in

To an innocuous address on Pinckney Street.
Now Lou the Loser uses all his ten
Thumbs to count up the minutes till she comes,
Or till (more likely, with his luck) she never shows.
The gin sets up a tickle in my toes.
I blow my nose. The room is hot. A fly
Does dead-stick landings on my neck. She's late.

3. *Three-Ten,* et seq.

The doorbell rings. I barrel down the stairs
To meet the coolest copy I have seen
Of Sally on the steps. Up in my room,
I fix her gin and secretly survey
This manifestation by which I have so
Astoundingly been visited: a girl.
She walks on her long legs, she talks out loud,
She moves her hand, she shakes her head and laughs.
Is this mechanical marvel to be mine?
Quite paralyzed, I nod and nod and nod
And smile and smile. The gin is getting low
In my tooth glass. The hour is getting on.
Gin and adrenalin finally rescue me
(With an assist from Sally) and I find
My lips saluting hers as if she were
My stern commanding officer. No fool,
She puts us on an equal footing. Soon
My strategies and tactics are as toys
Before the gallop of her cavalry
That tramples through my blood and captures me.

4. *Five-Fifty*

Later, as racy novels used to say,
Later, I turn to see the westering sun

Through the ailanthus stipple her tan side
With yellow coin dots shaped to fit her skin.
This Sally now does like a garment wear
The beauty of the evening; silent, bare,
Hips, shoulders, arms, tresses, and temples lie.
I watch her as she sleeps, the tapering back
Rising and falling on the tide of breath;
The long eyelashes lying on her cheek;
The black brows and the light mouth both at rest;
A living woman not a foot away.

The west wind noses in at the window,
Sending a scent of soap, a hint of her
Perfume, and the first onions of the night
Up the airshaft to where I lie, not quite alone.

Midsummer Night, Charles Street

The one untuned clock bell, ten minutes slow,
Tolls curfew for all tenants. The black bars
Exhale us into the dark street. Below,
The gutters swallow water; above, the stars

Roll in their ball race, bearing the dead weight
Of stricken hours below. Cancer, the Crab,
Surveys his citizens, who, huddled, wait
For the last word, the last light from a cab

To form our faces, the last touch of hands
Laid on our sleeves, the *dernier cri* of night.
We must ascend alone into the lands
Upstairs we live in. The initial flight

Is granite, which our crampons lace with sparks
Like kitchen matches'. The next flight is brick,
Glacé like ornamental walks in parks,
Offering no purchase to our pitons. Kick

A foothold in the sheer face, belay up
Over the lip of the third stage, rigid wood.
Last up a scant lath chimney to the top,
Where, sweated, scared, made up with dust and blood,

We face at length again the nightly sky,
Where our sign reigns alone, picking us out
Of our crowd on the Hill, who singly lie
About us in a similar case, no doubt.

Two Encounters

I. AT THE INN, 1947

Your mink scarf smells as if it smoked cigars,
And soot clings in the corners of your eyes,
And cold has cancelled your pale cheeks in red,
And you stand faintly in a veil of Joy,
And your kid gauntlet grips a round red bag,
And your lips taste of roses and Nestlé's
Milk-chocolate bars, and your long arms entail
My foreign body in the turning world.
One washroom later, in the oaken Inn
Where things transcend the bogus and return
To old simplicities aimed at and missed,
At least today, at least with you beside
Myself with love on the ridiculous
Oak settle picked as earnest of the past,
I see your color come back in the murk,
Drawn by a dark and blood-suborning drink.
I can't describe your long-shanked leverage
To move the world at that tart, flowery age:
The brief and just trial balance of your power.
However, I recall that at that hour —
After one drink, before the Dartmouth game —
You looked at me forever with an eye
Of tourmaline without a fleck or flaw,
Set in a mount of bone as plain as steel
And flesh as scanty and as beautiful
As a March pasture following rock ledge
Into a scythe of shadow, where the snow
Melts late, if ever. In that fixing glance

Framed by your hair as brown as beaver, I
Saw one faint faltering, one evidence
That even empires nod, that sceptres sway.

II.   AT THE FAIR, 1967

Dark lady of a dozen sonnets I
Endited in a winter and a spring,
We meet now in an altered circumstance
Across the floor far later in the dance —
Midnight approaches with its pumpkin car
To carry us away — and gravely tread
One tune together before partners change.
How you are changed and you are still the same:
Girl thirty-nine and woman twenty-one
Inseparably telescoped in one
Tall matron whose each mannerism rings
A dim bell in the back room of my mind.
With my wife and your daughter we attend
A spring fair: gangs of randy neon light
Seize your town common for one gaudy night
And set the Tilt-a-Whirl and Ferris wheel
Rotating to calliopes and screams
Above fluorescent grass. In the bookstall,
We find your former husband's fifteenth class
Report with Veritas stamped on its spine,
Price .25. His name does not appear.
Time shifts, but '47 was his year,
I think. Back in the pitch-black air
You ask me if I'll take a ride with you.
The Tilt-a-Whirl. Of course I will. The red
Sea of kid faces parts to let us through
And we sit in a narrow gondola,
Confined by a crossbar. The whirl begins:
First horizontally, then up and down.

Rim-tilted, lit in green and gold, the wheel
Drops out from under us. Kids yell.
I wince and grip the bar. I'm falling off.
What idiots! You laugh. I laugh and swear.
I'm really losing it. You grab my arm.
We laugh together, turning in the air,
Really alarmed, far too old to be here,
Glad when it ends and we can leave the park
After one night, like the fair, to the dark
We are accustomed to. Shaken, I'm glad
We did it, though. To hold your airborne arm
Twenty years later is to ride the calm
World's rim against the gravity of time.

Death City, 1949

(For C. A. S.)

Victorian urban redevelopers
Plotted a garden city for their hearse,
Drawn by four dapple greys, and its fast freight
Delivered from his home almost too late
But in the nick of time. Inveterate
Death dealers keep a large supply in stock,
All shapes and causes: falling, drowning, shock,
Birth and old age. Locust and Ash
Is the busiest corner in town, with the Cash
Memorial Block (of polished travertine)
Diagonally opposite the Lean
Spire, a split chocolate-covered brownstone fang.
On the next corner clockwise, the whole Lang
Family makes its white sepulchral home.
Finally, a pergola from Rome
(Grosser than Greece's) raises a Flaxman frieze
Over its rivals. On their marble knees,
Fat Vestals weep one who, the only son
Of a Senator, father of another one,
Was tantalized by the Pierian spring
Lifelong and died dehydrated. The thing
About this city is its arrogance,
Its cold assumption we would want to dance
To its dead march, sing to its dirge. Look out!
A Stygian barge appears and comes about
Two feet from us, its belly full of men, its black
Fluke raking us, its transom lettered Cadillac.
Charles, in a city where the only weeds

Are worn by widows, where the only deeds
Are done and done, they have no need of us.

Quitting a city which is dangerous,
Let us get on the Huron Avenue bus
And ride to our reprieve in love and pity
For the free burgesses of our death city.

Peg Finnan's Wake in Inman Square

At last his old nag's dead. In Finnerty's
Front parlor she looks up at the three-light
Pot-metal ceiling fixture, painted white,
While marble cake and whiskey are consumed
By Looney, Moriarty, Sweeney, Burke,
Costello, Mrs. Riordan, O'Rourke,
Ann Casey, Leary, Finnerty, McCue,
Finnan himself. He cries a tear or two
In freedom's honor and looks after her
As, rippleless, she slips away from shore
And puts a gulf between them, even while
Her brazen, toothless turtle's beak still smiles
With undertaker's rigor and her guile.
Finnan, unchained, still hears the passing bell
Of her bronze voice commanding him to tell
Why he was late, why he drank up his pay,
Why he forgot to bring her back *Screenplay,*
Why he missed Mass, why he made up to Dot
McCann on Inman Street, the dirty slut,
Why he got fired from Harty's. The last Pope,
A Sacred Heart, a cover from the *Globe*
Depicting John F. Kennedy look down
Upon their confrontation. Finnan's eyes,
Opaque and pale as first-communion skies,
Blink as he chases cake with whiskey. Out
He goes, unhampered, into a fall night
Of oak leaves on the move, and walks the street
Unsteadily toward the third-floor flat
Where he will drink his gin tonight alone,
In silence, free, poor fish, and far from home.

A Day in the City

(Boston — New York)

I. A TASTE OF QUEENS

The dead in Queens lean westward from their stones,
Bidding granitic and marmoreal
Adieux to their descendants, who go west
A better way across the bridge to lodge
Like unspent bullets in high offices
And spiring living rooms up in the air.
Low grow the tenant cabins, stucco, brick,
Half-timbered, double-numbered, where the quick
Who were not fast enough groom their feat sons
To leap the river, and, for love or money,
Fall stunningly upon the stony city.
Here Maple Towers (Now Renting 3-Rm. Apts.)
Now towers without a tree, its swimming pool
A blue oasis in the asphalt plain
Where caravans of Carey busses ply
From Flushing to their caravanserai
In that grey fret of city over there,
Bearing us strangers straight to our desire.

II. THE AMAIR TOWER

Amair, whose lightfoot jets transship today
Across the Pole to where tomorrow starts,
I do not like your *pied-à-terre* which squats,
Arrived and immemorial, upon
Diminished traces of that lovely grey
Novembrist town bespoke by the old school

Who specialized in rainy afternoons
Enclosing incandescent *thés-dansants,*
From which the singles and the couples went
On by tall lemon cab to their affairs
Down at the Cafe Brevoort or upstairs
Above the Plaza's tiles and palms. Now I
Am escalated to a mezzanine
From which I will be launched into an air —
Which fifty stories circulate — as rare
As the rich breath of couchant unicorns
Or levant chairmen at the dormant board,
Whose low end I will sit at and, like Molly,
Bloom into smiles and, yes, say yes to folly.

III.   HIGH PLACES

Sitting in conference with the president,
I am at first a trifle hesitant
To pierce his thin-skinned sphere with my harsh voice
And possibly dissipate his corporate choice
Of fruitwood furniture and cosmic view —
Look! Look! Canarsie! Inwood! Greenpoint! Kew
Gardens! United Nations Plaza! — true
Embodiment of everything that's ex-
Travagant in American life but sex,
Which is supplied in minims by Miss Hatch
Outside his office door to each fresh batch
Of clients, underlings, and impressees,
Who, on his bounty, sail the seven seas
Of his blue, black, calm, manic, angry moods,
This king of men and emperor of goods.
We talk across two tankards of his pale
Impeccable imported English ale,
Which break out in a fine cold sweat, like me,
In his stern presence. Can my dim words be

Reaching their destination? Yes, sir. He
Nods in his waking sleep and sanctifies
My views in every echelon of eyes.

IV.   EAST FORTY-SECOND STREET

Acutely, the late sun interrogates
The street held in its custody, casting
New light on western faces, shadowing
Each subject with the long arm of the law
Of relativity, gilding the back,
Benighting the east front of everyone.
In front of Longchamps, on a burning brass
Standpipe stained orange by sundown, a tall green
Girl worth her weight in meadows, orchards, trees
Sits waiting for her date to claim her long
Cool fall champaign, capped by black scuds of curls,
And stage a pastoral with her as Phyllis
And him as Colin, awkward, forward, witty,
Against the pre-cast forest of the city.

Sweeney to Mrs. Porter in the Spring

In Prospect Street, outside the Splendid Bar
And Grill, the Pepsi generation —
The beardless, hard-eyed future of our nation —
Rolls casually south out of the slum
From which it will go far,
Leaving an old country where spring has come.

It is not obvious about the spring.
You have to know the signs: a hoist of wash
On every back-piazza line, a sash
Propped open with an empty pint of cream,
A comic softening
Of the wind's blade to rubber, an old dream

Of something better coming soon for each
Survivor who achieves the shores of May —
Perhaps a legacy, a lucky play
At dogs or numbers, or a contest prize.
Lady Luck, on the beach
Between assignments, does not hear their cries,

"Me! Me!" like gulls'. She never will. The old
Diminish steadily in all but years
And hope, which, uncontrollable as tears,
Racks them with life. Just look at Mrs. Porter,
Preparing to unfold,
In the dark bar, a letter from her daughter,

A beauty operator in Ladue,
And to remasticate the lovely tale

Of ranch and Pontiac, washed down with ale
Cold from the Splendid bowels, while waiting for
Her unrefined but true
Love's shape to shade the frosted-glass front door.

Meanwhile, Sweeney, Medallion 83
(A low old-timer's number), wheels his hack,
In Independent livery, past a back-
Projected process shot of Central Square,
To where his love will be,
Impatient to resume their grand affair.

She, like a pile of black rugs, stirs to hear
His two-tone horn just outside, heralding
The coming of both Sweeney and the spring.
Inside, he greets her as before, "Hi, Keed,"
While Wilma lays his beer
And whiskey down between them and gets paid.

His knotty fingers, tipped with moons of dirt,
Lock on the shot of Seagram's, which he belts
And chases with a swig of Knick. Nobody else
Could comfort them except their old selves, who
Preserve, worn but unhurt,
The common knowledge of a thing or two

They did together under other moons.
Now the Splendid night begins again,
Unkinking cares, alleviating pain,
Permitting living memories to flood
This country for old men
With spring, their green tongues speaking from the mud.

On the Island

To an isle in the water
With her would I fly.
— *W. B. Yeats*

1. Friday Night

We issue from the meat of Pineapple Street,
Skipping in unison in the jet rain to
The cadence of our footsteps left behind
Just momentarily as we bound on
To water, laughing, soaked, four-legged and
Three-armed, two-hearted, Siamese, unique,
And fifty put together. On the Heights,
We embrace like trenchcoats on a rack at Brooks.
You taste like lipstick, wine, and cigarettes,
And, now quite irrecoverably, you:
A tear in the material of memory
No reweaver can match. Nevertheless,
I feel your rainy face against mine still,
Hear your low laugh join boat hoots in the night
(One Song, one Bridge of Fire! Is it Cathay?),
And see, just past the corner of your eye,
Our city momentarily at bay.

2. Saturday Morning

Starting for Paumanok from Remsen Street,
Taking my Buick, leaving your LaSalle,
Putting the top down in the false-spring light
Of February second, following
The "27" signs — Atlantic Ave.,
Rockaway Parkway, Linden Boulevard,

And Sunrise Highway finally at noon —
We leave the city we did sometime seek
In favor of the fish-shaped fastnesses
Due east, beyond the sounding wave
Of outer suburbs rushing up the shore
To flood the flat potato country with
The family of man. Past Babylon,
We run at last aground on the prewar
Simplicities and complications: farms
Looked down on by great houses in the style
Of Insull, piles of those who made a pile
In Motors, Telephone, and Radio,
And dropped it all down the defile
Between decades, where all our fortunes go.

3. Saturday Afternoon

Patchogue, my dear, offers a white-faced bar
With a black heart. In its interior
You are more beautiful than you really are,
More *dégagée,* more *jeux sont faits,* world-wearier.
That artificial night, with evident aim,
Plinks out my daylit thoughts and goes to black,
Where, in the tarry sky, the Bull, the Swan
Couple illegally till dawn
With lavish princesses and Spartan queens,
As I autistically do
With you, while you invent a terrible drink —
A pilot biscuit drowned in gin and It,
Dubbed a Wet Blanket, in a whisky glass —
Before my wondering eyes. With a bright crack,
A back door opens and the atmosphere
Of night blows out as sharply as a tire,
Revealing a slack rank of garbage cans
Out back, and a red carpet underfoot.

You look yourself again; I start to feel
Like death in the afternoon. Let us be gone.

4. Saturday Evening

Night, like a funeral, comes marching in
On muffled heels, its west-bent coffin met
By gathering naked bulbs and neon tubes
Along Sag Harbor's streets. Beyond the pale
Pearl light of day's regrettable demise
The whalers' churches and town halls rise up like white
Whales surfacing, their sugarloaves of white
Mammalian clapboards sailing on a grey,
Calm main of mud. These Puritanic arks,
Fane and profane, holy and secular,
Divide their flocks into white Sunday sheep,
Ripe to be fleeced of grace, and weekday goats,
Alert to steal their wool. A vesper bell,
Like a late bird, sings curfew to the town,
Turning our steps to where, in tongues of fire,
A stammering sign defines the Grande Hotel.

5. Saturday Night

Now, wearing my discounted wedding ring,
Still foggy with disuse, you face the desk,
Where the Korean War loudly bombards
The *Daily News* with black. The manageress,
A human hatchet in a florid dress,
Takes five from me for her best double. We
Go up and up to that sidereal
Address, where all the bentwood furniture,
The stunted metal bed, the chiffonier
Graced with our pint of Partners' Choice, but scarred
By all the post-coital cigarettes

Of sadder, wiser transients, the ashtray
("Momento of Peconic Bay"), the tin
Wastebasket lithographed with pennants, yours
Included, all call time and freeze till we
Move on. The four-light window, featuring
A huge streetlamp dead center, resonates
To the first wave of onshore rain as we
Resume our elevating, ludicrous
Posture of love. Dear Jane, the prize is far
Too near for me to melt with laughter now,
But there's a whoop down in my throat. Later,
And cooler, rubbing Lucky Strike ash in-
To my bare chest, I'll tell you what I mean:
The fact that I, unhandsome, awkward, pale,
And you, Vassar or no, too ample for
An age of skin and bone, should tumble for
Love seven stories high, with eyes as blue
As tropospheres, with dazzling teeth the size
Of cornerstones, and noses straight as dies:
The cliché of the first-class citizens.

6. *Monday Morning*

The party's over now. In a tense white
Ruffed blouse, you look as different from last night
As day. I swallow the last scratchy crumbs
Of my last baking-powder biscuit, and
Leave your place, touching for the first time now,
Noting my fingermarks on the front door.
Once more unto the breach: at the St. George
We sound the hellmouth of the I.R.T.
And ride the hissing, green, Draconic train
Under the river. *Wicker, wicker* goes
The air compressor at a stop. You sit
On shiny wicker, looking at my feet;

I hang from a chipped white-enamel strap
Marked Rico No. 12. Quite soon, at Wall
Street, we get off. Now leaving Trinity
Out of the corner of my eye, I spin
Behind you into the loud lobby of your tower
Where banks of Gothic elevators rise,
Absurd, on high. You turn and face me now,
All Bala-Cynwyd in your Peter Pan
Collar and single string of pearls, dear Jane.
"It's no go, Lou." "But wait —" "But why?" "But I —"
"I know, but it won't ever work. You know
That I have certain standards." "Pouring tea."
"Yes, pouring tea. And you just don't, that's all.
You just don't care." "But I can try." "Unh-uh.
Look, Lou, let's stop this." "Can't I see you once?
Just one more time? Tonight?" "No. I'll be late
For work upstairs. Goodbye." Now that I know
I won't see you again, an awful pain
Of deprivation twists my abdomen.
The lancet doors squeeze shut between us, and
Lights track your progress overhead as you
Devise me to myself. Jane, for the gift
Of you at first, then us, and lastly me,
My thanks, since even such off-islanders
As I can profit by a visit to
The fish-shaped island, population two.

Two

IV

The Tree Warden

I. A FAREWELL TO ELMS

In late July, now, leaves begin to fall:
A wintry skittering on the summer road,
Beside which grass, still needing to be mowed,
Gives rise to Turk's-caps, whose green tapering ball-
Point pens all suddenly write red. Last year,
The oriole swung his nest from the high fan
Vault of our tallest elm. Now a tree man
Tacks quarantine upon its trunk. I hear

An orange note a long way off, and thin
On our hill rain the ochre leaves. The white
Age of a weathered shingle stripes the bark.
Now surgeons sweat in many a paling park
And bone saws stammer blue smoke as they bite
Into the height of summer. Fall, begin.

II. THE SECOND EQUINOX

Perambulating his green wards, the tree
Warden sees summer's ashes turn to fall:
The topmost reaches first, then more, then all
The twigs take umbrage, publishing a sea

Of yellow leaflets as they go to ground.
Upon their pyres, the maples set red stars,
The seal of sickness unto death that bars
The door of summer. Bare above its mound

Of leaves, each tree makes a memorial
To its quick season and its sudden dead;

With a whole gale of sighs and heaving head,
Each ash attends its annual burial.

The warden, under a boreal blue sky,
Reminds himself that ashes never die.

III.   DECEMBER THIRTY-FIRST

The days drew in this fall with infinite art,
Making minutely earlier the stroke
Of night each evening, muting what awoke
Us later every morning: the red heart

Of sun. December's miniature day
Is borne out on its stretcher to be hung,
Dim, minor, and derivative, among
Great august canvases now locked away.

Opposed to dated day, the modern moon
Comes up to demonstrate its graphic skill:
Laying its white on white on with a will,
Its backward prism makes a monotone.

In the New Year, night after night will wane;
Color will conquer; art will be long again.

IV.   MAY DAY

Help me. I cannot apprehend the green
Haze that lights really upon the young
Aspens in our small swamp, but not for long.
Soon round leaves, as a matter of routine,
Will make their spheric music; and too soon
The stunning green will be a common place.

Sensational today runs in our race
To flee the might of May for willing June.

To reach a bunch of rusty maple keys,
Undoing a world of constants, more or less,
I tread on innocence. The warden sees
In May Day the historical success
Of labor; a safe date for planting trees;
A universal signal of distress.

String Song

And, if he then should dare to think
Of the fewness, muchness, rareness,
Greatness of this endless only
Precious world in which he says
He lives — he then unties the string.
                              — *Robert Graves*

I.

First, it is fundamental to realize
No two of anything may be alike.
That dawn out there that paints those loitering skies
Around St. Ceil's pale lemon, and tints white
Pilasters on its spire the tastiest lime,
Cannot come up the same another time
On morning's fruit machine, no matter how
Close the clock comes to telling the same hour.
The day shift moves the lingerers on now,
Into the shadow of the whited tower,
Whence they will not return another day
To interpret the same plot with the same play.

II.

A thousand bells belabor noon
And send it, beaten, to my room
On Canting Hill. I knock off work
And look out over Broome, Newkirk,
And Canterbridge, my mother's slum
From which my bleeding blessings come:
My ignorant and able art,
My aptitude to play the part

Of artist, my self-seeing eye.
Under the chimney-sweeping sky
Ten thousand houses smoke soft coal
And tap ash on my father's goal:
A terrace house exactly like
Ten thousand others, and a bike
Made by the gross in Brummagem.
In Milliard Street, our Hill's main stem,
I spy a hundred lines and queues
Of Catholics, Protestants, and Jews.
To work: now drying on the rack,
My sable brushes call me back
To carry out my grand designs
With infinite curlicues and lines.

III.

Looking straight down into Singleton Street,
I see one policeman tacking north in blue,
One Witness offering Watchtowers opposite,
One ray of sun striking my house askew,
One clock hitching itself, hand over hand, to six,
One couple walking south.
Allow me, as a colorist, to describe:
She wears an ivory Mackintosh, an alizarin hat,
Viridian pumps too good to eat. Her face is flesh.
His, on the other hand, is a tint of scarlet lake.
He wears an umber overcoat, jet shoes, a raw-sienna hat.
In shadow, all the tones are muddier;
In sunlight, all are biassed toward orange.
At this routine, immemorable moment,
The ragman's nag sways by with slow, arhythmic beats,
Pursued by cries of iron tires and "Rags!"
As usual on our street at six o'clock.

IV.

Just a black whisker in the top-right corner, and
My signature —"K. Zauber"— at the bottom, and
"The Way of the World" is done. The icy coffee in
The paper cup I hold in my cold, painted hand
Turns out to float a long-dead cigarette, which I
Almost ingest. The thing is done. I turn my back
On that dead square of canvas, which looks far too red
In incandescent light, and look out at the sky,
Now clamping down its curfew on all light resorts.
Night turns too solid places, squares, and terraces —
Thick cubic miles of intricate, Baroque decay —
Into an inverse star map which exhaustively reports
New constellations on a scale of one to one.
There is The Cloverleaf, where superhighways run;
There is Dad's Sunday Suit, three stars to form the fly;
There is The Steering Wheel, made of a rotary;
There is The Burning Cross in runway-marker lights;
There is The Model in the bosom of the Heights;
There is Self-Portrait, witty, pointed, populous
Abstraction of myself in the metropolis.

Our Literary Heritage

I. RIVERSIDE DRIVE, 1929

" 'Good-by, Ralph. It should end some other way.
Not this,' Corinna said. 'Now go away.'
No. Rhymes. It's ludicrous. Try 'Dear, good-by.'
No. Repetitious. Maybe 'Dear, farewell.'
No. Stagy. Out of character. Oh, hell.
Time for a drink." The Smith-Corona heaves
As he retracts his knickerbockered knees
To rise. Outside, a southbound tug receives
The sun broadside, and the bold Linit sign
Pales on the Jersey shore. Fresh gin, tk-tk-
Tk-tk-tk-tk, quite clearly fills his glass
Half full from the unlabelled bottle. Now
His boyish fingers grip the siphon's worn
Wire basketweave and press the trigger down
To utter soda water. One long sip
Subtracts a third of it for carrying.
On the way back, he pauses at the door
Beside his football picture, where a snore
Attests that all is well and promises
Him time to work. To work: before the tall,
Black, idle typewriter, before the small
Black type elitely inching on the blank
White sea of bond, he quails and takes a drink.
First, demolitions: the slant shilling mark
Defaces half a hundred characters
With killing strike-overs. Now, a new start:
" 'Good-by, Ralph. I don't know why it should end
Like tihs,' Corinna said. 'But be my freind.' "

II. HOTEL SHAWMUT, BOSTON, 1946

(From a commercial travellers' hotel,
Professor S. jumped straight down into hell,
While — jug-o'-rum-rum — engines made their way
Beneath him, one so cold December day.)

While he prepares his body, cold gears mate
And chuckle in the long draught of the street.
He shaves; his silver spectacles peruse
An issue of *The North American Muse*.
He uses Mum; outside him in the hall,
Maids talk their language; snow begins to fall.
He puts on his old clothes. The narrow room
Has nothing, nothing to discuss with him
Except what time you should send out your suit
And shoes for cleaning. Now he stamps his foot:
Outside the window, not saying anything,
Appears a seagull, standing on one wing;
A long-awaited colleague. With glad cry,
Professor S. embraces the white sky.

While S. demolishes a taxicab,
His spectacles review the life of Crabbe.

(From a commercial travellers' hotel,
Professor S. descended into hell.
But once in April in New Haven he
Kissed a friend's sister in the gloom of trees.)

III. DEUS EX MACHINA, FLUSHING, 1966

La Guardia. Knee-deep in storyboards,
I line up for the shuttle, which arrives

Outside the gate and off-loads shuffling streams
Of transferees — each in his uniform
Of sober stuff and nonsense, with a case
Of talents at his side — who pass our line
Of sombre-suited shuttlers carrying
Our cases on. Then one appears, a rare
Bird in migration to New York, a bare-
Crowned singer of the stony coast of Maine,
And of Third Avenue in rain; a bard.
The way of the almost-extinct is hard.
He peers through tortoise-shelly glasses at
The crowd, the place, the year. He is not here
And is. In his check jacket, he describes
An arc of back and arms as he proceeds
Between two city starlings, carrying
His store of songs in a beat leather grip
And a dried drop of his brown lamb's blood on
His wilted collar. A *Time*-reader in
Glenurquhart plaid identifies his bird —
"Godwit, the poet"— to a flannel friend.
The bard stalks on on his two legs, aware
He has been spotted; in, I'd say, some pain
At an existence which anticipates
Its end and in the meantime tolerates
Intolerance of the wing, the whim, the one
Unanswerable voice which sings alone.

IV. LAMENT FOR THE MAKERS, INCLUDING
      ME: 1967

New-minted coin, my poet's mask
(A small denomination in
Demotic nickel, brass, or tin)
Passes from hand to hand to hand
Beyond my six acres of land.

Did I desire such currency
Among the meritocracy
Of tri-named ladies who preserve
The flame of art in mackled hands,
Of universitarians
And decimal librarians
Who shore and store up textual
Addenda, of asexual
Old arbiters and referees
Who startle letters with a sneeze,
Of critics whose incautious cough
Halts a new wave or sends it off
To break on uninhabited shores,
Of publishers, insensual bores
Procuring art —"A maidenhead!"—
To Jack the Reader, of well-read
Young underfaced admirers who
Impinge on undefended you
At readings in all colleges?
No, I did not; but knowledge is
All-powerless to seek redress
For injuries to innocence.
I think continually of
Abjurers, who, fed on self-love,
Housed in an incommodious cave,
Clothed in three-button sackcloth, crave
Indulgence of no audience
But their own laudatory ears.
Alack, this anchoritic few
Dwindles; these ticking times are too
Struck with celebrity's arrears,
And heap past-due advances on
The embryonic artisan;
All hours from dawn to night are lauds,
All auditors are all applause

(However electronic), all
Tempters conspire in Adam's fall.

The world turned upside-down, without
A beast in view, without a doubt,
Recalls its exiles and bestows
On them the palm, the bays, the rose
(Art sick?), the Laurel Wormser Prize,
Whose debased dollar only buys
More nods, more goods, more fame, more praise:
Not art, as in the rude old days.

Now worldward poets turn and say,
Timor vitae conturbat me.

Just a Whack at Empson

We rot and rot and rot and rot and rot.
Why not cut badinages to the bone?
Alas, cockchafers cuddle. We cannot.

We recognise the hand upon our twat;
Unfortunately X is always known.
We rot and rot and rot and rot and rot.

Unfortunately X is always not
Quite what we had in mind to end our moan.
Alas, cockchafers cuddle. We cannot.

Why must we be contained within our pot
Of message which we have so long outgrown?
We rot and rot and rot and rot and rot.

Your physic beauty made my inwards hot
Whilst talking to you on the telephone.
Alas, cockchafers cuddle. We cannot.

Each greening apple has its browning spot:
"The rank of every poet is well-known."
We rot and rot and rot and rot and rot.
Alas, cockchafers cuddle. We cannot.

Dear George Orwell, 1950-1965

Dear George Orwell,
I never said farewell.
There was too much going on:
Crabgrass in the lawn
And guests to entertain,
Light bantering with pain
(But wait till later on),
Love nightly come and gone.
But always in the chinks
Of my time (or the bank's),
I read your books again.
In Schrafft's or on the run
To my demanding clients,
I read you in the silence
Of the spell you spun.
My dearest Englishman,
My stubborn unmet friend,
Who waited for the end
In perfect pain and love
And walked to his own grave
With a warm wink and wave
To all; who would not pull
The trigger on the bull
Elephant, and who,
Seeing his foe undo
His pants across the lines,
Did not blow out his brains;
Who served the Hôtel X
As low man, slept in spikes

With tramps, in Rowton Houses
With pavement artists, boozers,
Boys, insomniacs;
Who spat on shams and hacks,
Lived in a raddled flat
Passing trains hooted at,
And died for what we are.
Farewell, Eric Blair.

Peace Comes to Still River, Mass.

Down at Fort Devens guns begin again:
I hear the thirties rattle, and the thin
Patter of rifles, each manned by a man
Invisible, disposable, and in
Our first line of defense, the paper says.
Now howitzers inflame our darkling days,
Exclaiming downrange in an O of fire
Upon their targets, and a virid flare
Gives the high sign to go on making war
In earnest of our inner truce. Once more
My quondam dean in University Hall
Stands in the breach of peace, whence he will call
Down fire on the bald, woolly heads of all
Professors of the other point of view,
Who, flanked and enfiladed and too few,
Will soon throw down their dated arms, of course,
And yield themselves to a superior force
Of well-drilled intellectual police,
Sworn on our honor to enforce the peace.

Chamber Music, Bar Harbor, Off-Season

Vivaldi's pizzicato winter falls
On my bared head, as on the tangerine
Tiles overhead, with a soft pluck that calls
Off summer, plain and Indian, to bring
On All-American autumn, full of tears
For all America's bright college years.
An instance: take this mouldering hotel,
Built as a monstrous cottage by a swell
Manhattan traction millionaire in 1910,
And now far past its hour; or take this room,
This second chamber: nobs bathed in its long,
Crazed tub with nickel fittings, and were clothed
In white tie, studs, and pumps by a slight man
(The Unknown Servant), and went down to dine.
Was not their bravery of living fine?
The closet holds a lockbox for their jewels;
The ceiling is as high as their desires;
The fireplace, dead, is ample for their fires;
The bed and desk conform to their taut rules.
Outside, the maples shed stars in the pools
On the decedent lawn. The chamber group
Strikes up its water music on the roof
Encore, fretting fleeting, immutable
Silver-toned strings tuned at the cedar eaves,
Bowed by the balustrade, frayed on the ground.
Likewise impermanent and perpetual,
What will we leave half as ebullient,

Triumphal, potent, personal as this
Old place, old pergola, old hearth, old house?
Roll on, then, fall, sole death we can remember,
Routing the summer in our rented chamber.

V

The Marschallin, Joy Street, July 3, 1949

> Manchmal hör' ich sie fliessen —
> unaufhaltsam.
> Manchmal steh' ich auf mitten in der Nacht
> und lass die Uhren alle, alle stehn.
> — *Hofmannsthal,* Rosenkavalier

> The penal gaol of Mountjoy, gaol 'em and joy.
> — *James Joyce*

1.

At 2200 hours, a silver flare
Profusely illustrates the western air,
Sending poor Mona Mountjoy to the heights
Of her tall town house overlooking Joy
And Pinckney Streets. Her long and shapely brown
Hands, dusted with the first faint liver spots
As if by accident, pick up her husband's Zeiss
Night glasses and range in on Harvard Square,
Bearing 290 at ten thousand yards.
Fire one! A small white integer appears,
Bears a huge school of yellow pollywogs,
And, with a white wink, vanishes. The boom
Takes twenty-seven seconds to arrive
Across East Cambridge as the crow flies. Now
A star shell bursts northeast. Dim in the south,
Dorchester Heights replies, and at her feet
The Common coughs up its first rocket of the night,
A red stem blooming in an amber star,
Which splits (by fission) into asterisks
As numerous and green as grass. At last
Her Major General has gone west tonight

(Though only literally), riding in a Jeep
Like any of his boys, and soon will sleep
Or lie, not unaccompanied, in the red
Light of a motel sign in Plattsburgh, where
He bivouacs for the morning march to Drum.

2.

The Major General is gone; alas,
Without replacement. Ian Quinn tonight
Is racing for Bermuda in the moon
Which rises earlier for seafarers
Bound east. Northwest, an imitation moon
Sails over Cambridge and divides itself
Impartially in seven satellites
White as the Pleiades. A Common sun
Rim-lights her long face with its Sayward nose
And dark-blue Dunster eyes. A river wind
Stirs her half-silver hair, switches her dress
Around her knees, whistles a winter air
Among the guy wires. Dimly, deep downstairs,
A doorbell rings beneath the rocketry,
And Anna goes to answer. At this hour
Who would walk up the steep side of Joy Street
To call on her? Bad news? A telegram?
A yellow pang? No, now they use the 'phone.
She steps into the black trap to the top
Story, her long legs in up to the knee;
Then she is a tall torso, and then she
Takes her blond disembodied head below.
The dark fifth-story boxroom is still hot.
A fan croons in the maid's room on the fourth.
Her own third-floor bedroom is dark and still.
The upstairs parlor is lit by one lamp.
The downstairs one contains her husband's Uncle Will.

3.

Returning, he says (over a long Scotch
Which he has made himself, apparently),
Returning from a meeting at the Union Club
Of the Parnassian Sodality
(Where, with his classmates of the Class of '94,
He sang, "Drink to Me Only with Thine Eyes,"
"We'll Go No More A-Roving," and, to close,
"Fair Harvard," in his obbligato voice);
Returning across Beacon and up Joy
Toward his little flat in Myrtle Street,
He thought to stop and call upon his niece,
And tell her his good news. (Out of one eye
She spies his dog-eared yellow calling card
On Anna's silver tray.) Good news indeed:
Will has determined to become betrothed,
At last, at last, to a lady of family.
One Mona knows; a famous beauty; young.
(He punctuates his points with a gold cane.)
In fact, Will says, his trustee's voice a thread
Of cunning whispering out of his starred face:
In fact, he is effecting nothing less
Than one more union of the Mountjoy line
With, — yes, the Saywards. Here is her picture,
Which a few hours ago at a *rendez-vous*
She pressed into his hand; her miniature.
Mona takes the smudged half-column cut
Clipped from this morning's *Herald* society page.
"Post-deb," it says, "assists at fashion tea."
The girl is Sally Sayward, her own niece.
His eyes as blue as starry chicory flowers
In vacant lots, his purple smile as warm
As summertime, his manners beautiful

As any plate in *Godey's Lady's Book,*
He rises now to take his leave. "Enough,
My dear, of my good news. I must be off.
Good night, good night." Above Will's trilby hat,
The roof of Pinckney Street is shot with fire.

4.

The fireworks are not done. She goes upstairs
To her housetop again. A grunt of rain
Clouds in the west announces the intent
Of the deluge to fall on schedule,
As promised on the radio. The Park
Commissioners of Cambridge show at last
The color of their money in a green,
Red, azure, nude, cerise, and chartreuse blast,
Whose elegant ballistics shame the moon.
Its third stage, firing, adumbrates the flank
Of the first nimbus cloud, whose sheer freeboard
Goes straight up twenty-seven thousand feet,
Past cumulus to cirrus. She remarks
The coolness of its first forerunning winds,
Their spearheads bypassing strong points of heat.
On such a night she met the General,
Disguised as Minot Mountjoy, bond broker,
Concealing the identity of the head
Of Hall & Mountjoy; equally disguised
As Captain Mountjoy of the 26th,
Whose olive shoulderboards sustained the pips
Which would grow into the commanding stars
Of 26th Division, National Guard,
Through the good offices of thirty years.
On such a night in 1922,
She met Mountjoy in summer's high estate,
An awkward Sayward daughter now a swan,

A beauty twenty, and imprisoned him
With her short blond bob and her long dark laugh,
As he imprisoned her in the high place
She occupies alone on Joy Street now.

5.

Someplace, apparently Arlington, begins
Its own fire fight in the northwest. On such
A night, too, she met Ian Quinn. In June,
The Eastern Yacht Club is lit up at night
With amber lanterns where the members dance
Indoors and out; there, just two years ago,
She first danced with him. In the low light, she
Carried her forty-five years well; and he,
Worn with ten years at sea and four at war,
Looked older than his thirty-three. Two years,
Two years now they have occupied plotting
To intersect their courses on a chart
Awash with obstacles: stubborn routines
Running abysmally deep; mutual friends
Marking their channel everywhere like rocks;
Exhausting care and caution forming bars
To their resolve. (Against this set the shock
Of his hands on her bare arms in the dark
Hotel room after a month's absence, or
The quick kiss —"Watch my lipstick!"— at her door,
Containing a month's worth of intimacy.)
Nevertheless, the end is perfectly clear.

6.

Its magazines hit by a lucky shot,
The first cloud bursts into internal fire,
Suddenly started, suddenly put out.

When will his skillful, luckless shot hit her?
Soon. Only this morning, in her hand mirror,
She read between the lines state's evidence
Amassed by forty-seven years. No doubt
She dreamt again last night of waking in the small
Of the night's back and stopping all the clocks,
Upstairs and down, because she could not bear
To hear time running through its tidemarks. All
The signs are negative; the hour glass drops
To storm point; still the thunderheads come on.

7.

The Common finishes its business
For one more year with an immense barrage
Of small white rockets with a terrier's sharp
And penetrating bark. In the bright lights
Of their impermanent sky sign can be seen
One tear in her eye, to memorialize
The fact that one day, now, tomorrow, or
Next year, he will leave her for someone else
Younger and prettier, as her glass predicts.
Stupid to speculate: but if she had
Her wrenching wish, it would be Sally Sayward,
Her gawky niece irradiating love,
Her silly self at twenty over again.

8.

Before its time, chain lightning makes next day
Out of tonight, then fuses all its lights
With a white snick and a black avalanche,
Burying here and now and far away.
So time utters an annual report,
Heard loud and clear, on its last fiscal year

In the man market, on its day-to-day
Quotations, on its gains in brick and clay,
Its wins on the Exchange and in the Court
Of No Resort. The last man-made stars burn
Out in the west, the last spectacular
Dwindles to darkness in the captured fort.
The dandelions of light now go to seed.
In Joy Street, Mona Mountjoy, like the year,
Ends her summation and begins to turn
Toward the dockets of more pressing need:
A house to keep, a failure to hold dear,
A fiction to maintain, another year
To fill with guest appearances, each day
Farced full, penned black and blue, marked with a mort
Of dates, engagements, living tongues to learn
At Berlitz, trips to take, and friends to mourn.
Being herself, she takes it well indeed;
She has had all the fireworks she will need.
She goes belowstairs, an unbroken reed,
To put her windows down against the rain.

VI

A Common Prophecy

Crossing the Common, instep-deep in leaves,
To see my man for governor, I hear
A stentor's voice across the amber sheaves
Of summer underfoot: a drone of fear

That could be newsboys heralding a war
Whose front might coincide with Tremont Street,
Knocking each English elm and Colonel Shaw
Into a cocked hat at my marching feet,

Which now tread out the vintage where the grapes
Of drought are stored for our posterity.
I isolate the voice. In marble drapes
Of muslin, on a platform of asperity —

A green bench — a white-headed sibyl stands
And damns us all. "Boston will be destroyed,"
She screams in a deep tenor, and her hands
Ring down our likely curtains from the void.

Bethlehem State

In durance soundly cagèd
On the lordly lofts of Bedlam,
With stubble soft and dainty,
Brave bracelets strong, sweet whips ding-dong,
With wholesome hunger plenty.

— *Old Song*

Et les moins sots, hardis amants de la Démence,
Fuyant le grand troupeau parqué par le Destin. . . .

— *Baudelaire*

I. GERSON

You smile with all the irony of life,
Showing your teeth, on the stupidity
Of your unsubtle keepers. How can they
Use locks and laws to be your masters, these
Trusties and toadies, lackeys, state-lovers?
How can you bear such ciphers, noughts and crosses?
How can the bossed become their betters' bosses,
Saying, Now brush your teeth, it's time to dress,
Go to the toilet, meet your visitors?
No, no. These beefy clowns with broken veins
Across their faces, waxy, bony doctors
Who squat on some dark secret, flat-faced nurses
Abandoned to some shady appetite
Are nasty, brutish, short compared to you.
Your towering rages raise you high above
This sane and dwarfish rabble of your peers,
Or, anyway, contemporaries, who,
Seeing your danger, put you in your place
In the brown air of Bethlehem, compost
Of ethyl alcohol, warmed-up pot roast,
Sweat, rubber tile, and unclean urinals,

Gravy, mothballs, stale flowers, and funerals,
Where corridors connect with corridors,
And yellow halls run on to intersect
In interborough fissures of the mind;
Where, through a guarded door of steel, I find
You in the violent ward, as meek and mild
As any christom child, as my roommate
Of seven years ago. That was before
You packed more wings and spurs than I and flew
Onward and upward into the wild blue
Beyond where I could breathe in the thin air,
And melted in the sun and landed here.
Ah, Noah Gerson, grounded from your gross
Fugue into fancy, meet the plain people,
The drones who drag their bourdon out for life
And drown your voluntary. But you're safe:
They're all behind locked doors, and you sail on,
Still captain of your heart, aboard this ark
Whose passengers are your fellow-animals:
Rough beasts who slouched to Bethlehem to die,
Mild innocents immaculately conceived,
Old men, all veins, who babble of green fields,
Young fathers, short-haired mad executives.
Bon voyage, Noah, over a lost world.

II.   BETHLEHEM

O little town of Bethlehem, N.Y.,
One Christmas past, another present, I
Stand once again on Cedar Mountain, and
Look down upon the old town which looks down
On the old Hudson from its barefaced bluff,
Whose summit brandishes Bethlehem State,
All cloud-capped mouse towers which encapsulate
Another of my fortune's hostages

Without a ransom note. Small, bitter snow
Ticks on my hatbrim, and the lights come on
At the end of another year in the toy town —
The red-and-green strings on the Bluevelt Street
Dime stores, a Santa Claus beneath my feet
In Rikerstown, a twinkling of lit trees
Up north in Haversack, and one magic
Pure-red festoon over the gilded name
Board of the old Columbiana Hose
Company No. 1 in Clinton Street.
Above its palisade, the hospital
Contributes "Merry Xmas" in white lights
Across its cruel and fanciful façade,
Whose dark, suggestive, and aberrant powers
Now toll me to its halls for visiting hours.

III.   DR. CRANKHITE

Fourteen-foot-high ceilings. Mission oak.
Dooms of dark woodwork. Under one green lamp,
The rosy Doctor glows and stirs for me.
"Chief, Psychiatric Service," his nameplate
States, shaming me and my A.B. His hands
Manipulate a concertina made
Out of thin air as he explains, squeezing
Roomfuls of theory into pleasing
Musique concrète (which practicing perfects)
And drawing out, conversely, such sustained
Notes on the patient as would make a text,
And will, and will. But in mid-chord he stops,
Rapt on the podium before my eyes,
And ducks his knowing head and nods and sighs
"Electric shock," as cool as Boreas.
The chill freezes my face as he explains
Why, when our interest and patience flag,

Black magic is plugged in to stun the brain
And punish the offender. "Much improved.
Increasing manual skills. Depression, less.
Social adjustment, better. Danced last week.
On Tuesday, drew. All for the best. What else
Was there to do?" What else, what else? Thank you.

IV.   MRS. EDWARDS

"O.K., Mr. Edwards, sit in here.
They'll have her down real soon." Ten minutes with
A coverless *Collier's* on the chill sun porch
Beside a spineless two-foot paper tree
With cardboard ornaments, and then I see
Her standing in the doorway, suddenly
Distant, diminished, vanished from herself,
Translucent, fragile, thin, invisible
The way she was short days ago. She sits,
A bird beside me on the wicker couch,
Shy, starving, who has put herself in danger
To take bread at my hand. And now I range
Over the pitiful subject matter I
Will be allowed to cover, hearing my
Words falling hollow down a well. She smiles,
As weathered as the winter sun which stands
Unmoved upon its solstice, as I hand
Her my square present in gold foil, which she
Cannot undo for her gross tremor. So
I open it to show the silver beads.
"They're beautiful. I'll put them on." Above
The issue bathrobe two sizes too big,
Below her thin and institutional
Cheek, on her young girl's neck, the necklace is
Stunningly wrong. What business has
Christmas coming around here, anyway?

Committed to forever and a day,
These inmates need no presents to destroy
The aimlessness of their routine, no holiday
To grant them crushing hope, no visitors
To exercise their wounds. It's time. She turns away
With a faint phrase I can't quite catch, and pads,
Beside her matron, down the vasty hall
Toward her quarters, till she is a small
White figure one in the far distance, where
We cannot touch each other any more.

Sondra Dead or Alive

I. CAMBRIDGE, 1955

The trouble was nobody laughed at her
Too witty poems when she read in 5
Harvard Hall. Professor Dix was there.
He smiled. Hardly a man is now alive.

Nevertheless, she is the talk of the town.
Or gown, at least. Divinity Avenue
Is bathed in her florescence. Down around
Memorial Drive she is a *succès fou*.

In her garden last night I laughed. Alas, too late.
I am afraid it came in the wrong place.
A poetess defends her puny kit
Fiercer than tigresses. Witness my face.

How can we classify this astonishing piece
Of resistance? Her underground effrontery
Is now quite superficial; underneath
The loud whalebone she is a quiet country.

Perhaps. Sumner, her husband, does not say
Word one. Burdened, he sometimes sighs.
Transfixed by his prize catch, day after day
He eats her with his macroscopic eyes.

II. LE TOMBEAU DE SONDRA MANN

Outside the Ritz, half-past our fifth Martini
With a twist I hand you into your Healey,

Returning your spirituous kiss, not really
Caught in your gin as you turn up Newbury.

The blat of your exhaust scatters the leaves
Of a December *Herald* underfoot;
For halt pedestrians you give a hoot
And pop the clutch in potently, O brave

And disappearing racer, all too soon
Vanished beyond the end of Berkeley Street.
Now, queen and huntress in a bucket seat,
How come I pace your grave in the new moon?

ENVOY

As I sat in the Ritz-Carlton, drinking the crystal wine,
And outside in the world the old moon died, a silver rind,
They told me you were dead, chauffeur, and I, for auld lang syne,
Took one more cup of kindness for the coldness that was mine.

Man and Wife

You were a unit when I saw you last:
The handsome husband and the happy wife,
Which was an act; but tissue of the past
Between you, unseen, made you one for life,

Or so I thought. It seems that I was wrong.
Seeing you ten years later, the kids grown
And gone, the still light of the long
Living room coming between you, I should have known

The lines were down. Your life went on with such
Attention to unchange: each "darling" fell
With metered carelessness; each "please" with much
Conviction; each "thanks" rang true as a bell.

But when you walked me to the door to go,
I saw the fault between your faces. Oh.

Two Happenings in Boston

I. A DISAPPEARANCE IN WEST
CEDAR STREET

Did Shriner die or make it to New York?
In his side room, across the hall from mine,
Wide windows air bare ticking. On a line
Outside, clean sheets flap. Samples of his work

Litter the closet: a barbed, wiry nude
In his hirsute pen line; a sketch of me
In ink and wash; a torn gouache of three
Pears on a windowsill. A cache of food —

Saltines, Velveeta Cheese, dried apricots —
Hid in a cairn of bags is now laid bare.
Also a bathrobe belt, one sock, a pair
Of sneakers with frayed laces tied in knots,

A paperback "Candide." Did Shriner die
While I was on the Cape? Did his cough stop
Dead in the welfare ward? Did a blue cop
Wheel Shriner out under the summer sky?

Did absolutely nobody appear
When they interred his box in Potter's Field?
(*I* would have been there.) Did nobody yield
A summer hat, a winter thought, a tear?

Or did he make it to New York? Did his
Ship dock at last at Fifty-Seventh Street?

Did angels, agents, and collectors meet
His price for life? Is that where Shriner is?

Does he sit down now in Minetta's late
With mistresses and models on each hand?
And is he now an icon in the land
Of mind and matter southward of Hell Gate?

Grey curtains flutter. A tall smell of pork
Ascends the stairs. The landlady below
Tells me in broken English she don't know.
Did Shriner die or make it to New York?

II.   A READING IN HUNTINGTON AVENUE

Hernando Milton, scion of the grey
Daylight that realizes all the stale
Unprofitable flats of the Fenway,
Halftone from head to foot, beyond the pale

Of ordinary people, reads his play
Aloud in the Alliance of the Arts,
Heard out by the dried flower of the Back Bay,
In moulting foxes, as he takes all parts.

That phalanx of once-marbled womanhood
Whose forties closed their minds and shut their hearts
Adores to hear the son of the late good
Nan Makepeace, sadly laid low by the darts

Of two degenerative diseases; lewd
Behavior by her disappearing husband, missed
Alone by whisperers; extremely rude
News of her son; and one obituarist.

Hernando Makepeace Milton, known as Nan
(Just like his mother) to a little list
Of boys on Beacon Hill, reads with élan
To the foxed ladies who will miss the gist,

With luck, of his verse play, entitled "Pan
And Hemp," and wholly dedicated to
The keen sensations of a happy man
(Himself) while smoking hashish. No one who

Savors the sound of words like a devotee
Of the Alliance of the Arts dare do
More than lie back and let a lurid sea
Of tone colors ravish her hair-do.

The baby-blue spot points to the last dance
Spun out by Milton, whose whole face is blue
With that light and the onset of a trance
Of *cannabis indica*. The play comes true.

Provincetown, 1953

The terns and seagulls tremble at your death
In these home waters.
— *Robert Lowell*

I. BACKS OF THE CAPE

Two people couple on the beach. Above,
A fish crow flies his pattern in a stack
Of seagulls, seeing flesh as carrion
On the flat sand below, between the blue
Brim of the ocean and its undertow,
And the drab green of scrub among the dunes.
The wind is west and hot. A charter boat
Winks on the outline of the world, and sand
Blows over rusty rails inshore. The white
Brick lighthouse on the point must wait for night
To say its message, though bare bodies flash
Their heliograph across broad day. Sea salt,
Sweat salt cement them, each to each, upon
The bright beach towel, and breath comes thicker till
Her legs lock, loosen, lock upon his legs,
And their love falls apart upon the sand,
Crossed by the shadow of one circling crow.

II. COMMERCIAL STREET

No weathered clapboard or white-painted stone
Is left unturned to profit in this old
Arcade of follies where fat trippers dodge
Long summerers in sneaks and amputee
Tan chinos severed far above the knee,

Who in their turn duck party-faced recruits
Straight from West Eighth Street in their chukka boots,
Who also *dos-à-dos,* this time with spare
Maids of the Cape who, single, mind the store
Less, on the whole, than liberties from their
Fresh boy friends lettered "P.H.S." The Pier
Offers escape through Off-Street Parking to
Some fishy old romance of tarry smacks
Champing at anchor in a lavender
Sea of dead squid trapped by the tide; but here,
Trammelled on every hand by souvenirs
And overseen by the grim Monument
(Upended splinter of a Romanesque
High school in Heidelberg, P.A.) and by
The Manor, borne up by its class of guest —
A summer swallow in a Madras vest —
And riding high on its paint Plimsoll line
Of freshness, we must face the peeling town:
Skeletal, florid, crass, alluring, dull,
Spontaneous, premeditated, whole.

III.   MANN'S PLACE

"Have you met Sondra?" "The entablature
Is filled with generals in relief." "I said, 'Look —
You can just shove your fellowship.' " "I love
That yellow maillot. Saks?" "The Pleistocene
Or earlier." "No. Double bitters." "Ham
Has played the Cherry Lane." "A Ford V-8."
"He had this great dead fish, my dear." *"Solfège."*
"No. She was Peter's cousin." "You have such
Astonishing green eyes." " 'Stuprate, they rend
Each other when they kiss.' " "No, please, no more
For me." "You just try teaching 101."
"Pure crimson lake." "Fourth down and two to go

And getting dark." "Say, who's your friend?" "Casals
Just swallows you in tone." " 'I do not hope
To turn again.' " "Oh, Harry's not so bad."
"Shut up." "There's something calm about you." "Where?"
" 'At the first turning of the second stair.' "
"Please, Michael, don't." "The Louvre." "Let's go outside."
"Her diction stinks." "My analyst just died."

IV.   THE KING ON A BIKE

Kings, queens, and aces shuffle on the scarred
Deck of the dance floor, drawing to each pair
The poker faces at the tables, where
Each name or number waits the call to dance
The permutations of the draw, the chance
To join another in a game of bluff
Against the world, which sees or calls enough
Sooner or later so we win or lose.
But now the operative term is choose:
One's dress, one's step, one's love, one's mind, one's mask
(Unfrightening, unlike one's face), one's task
To be evaded or embraced for life,
Erect, immutable, the stainless knife
That shapes us to a point or pares us down.

V.   RACE POINT: $5 PLANE RIDE

Down-ocean from our climbing Piper Cub
And its flat shadow skipping over dunes,
Skimming the yellow shallows of lagoons,
Skirting the ocean, green, blue-green, and blue,
The girl in our plane's belly sights a grey
Great tadpole shape and shouts, "A whale! A whale!"
A whale, indeed, proceeds across our tail
In keel-deep water, one infrequent fluke

Just punting him along. A whale: a fluke
Of ocean to remind the Cape people
Of the eroded point of the harpoons
Which rust above their mantels. The sole whale
Patrolling his home waters, the white light
Which signals the sand's end, the ultimate
Stone shack with two-throat foghorns on its rock,
All serve historic functions: statues all,
Alive or not, commemorate this point's
Last turn from the saline concerns of sea —
Fish, ships, storms, fresh names in the cemetery —
To the demands of land and their supply.

VI.   EPILOGUE: ROUTE 6

Only the contact patches of our tires —
Sixty square inches — bind us to the world
Which we pass over lightly late at night.
Route 6 unreels its story line in white
Morse dashes on a static brook of black.
Faint bluffs corroborate the presence of
A planet under us. In the dash light —
If I should dare to turn my head — I'd see
Who you are with me, whether blond or brown,
Blue-eyed or otherwise, plain, handsome, thin,
Short, tall, or in-between. Between us fall —
Across the strait tan seat of my M.G. —
Sands of the dunes of anonymity
Where we are set to track a barren mate,
A desert passenger whose drifted face,
An undeciphered stone, may be the one:
A matter of indifference to the sun.

VII

The West Forties:
Morning, Noon, and Night

> But nothing whatever is by love debarred.
> *— Patrick Kavanagh*

I. WELCOME TO HOTEL MAJESTY
(SINGLES $4 UP)

On this hotel, their rumpled royalties
Descend from their cross-country busses, loyalties
Suspended, losses cut, loves left behind,
To strike it lucky in the state of mind
That manufactures marvels out of mud.
Ensanguined by a bar sign selling Bud,
The early-streamline lobby — in its shell
Of late-Edwardian ornament, with a bell-
Mouthed cupidon extolling every swag
On its tall, fruitful front (a stale sight gag
First uttered by the comic landsmen who
Compounded a Great White Way out of blue
Sky, gneiss, and schist a whole stone age ago,
Before time steeled the arteries we know) —
The lobby washes redly over guests
With rope-bound bags containing their one best
Suit, shirt, tie, Jockey shorts, and pair of socks,
Half-empty pint, electric-razor box,
Ex-wife's still-smiling picture, high-school ring,
Harmonica, discharge, and everything.
Amid the alien corn and ruthless tares,
I hear a royal cry of horseplayers
Winding their tin horns in a chant of brass,
Their voices claiming in the wilderness.

II. SAL'S ATOMIC SUBMARINES

The Puerto Rican busboy, Jesus, coughs
Above the cutting board where Sal compiles
An outbound order for the Abinger
Associates next door; then, carrying
A pantheon of Heroes in a brown
Kraft-paper bag, he sidles by the chrome-
Formica-plastic dinette furniture
And gains the world, where anti-personnel
Gasses from crosstown busses, vegetable
Soup simmering at Bickford's, and My Sin
Seeping from Walgreen's silently combine
To addle all outsiders. Only lithe,
Quick indigenes like Jesus (whose tan neck
Is thinner than my wrist) can long survive
And later even prosper in the air
Of these times' squares, these hexahedral hives
Where every worker bustles for his Queen.

III. PENNY ARCADIA

Like lava, rock erupts to fill the room
From each coäx-, coäx-, coäxial
Concentric speaker's throat, and rolls like doom
Over the unmoved pinball-playing boys,
Whose jaws lightly reciprocate like long-
Stroke pistons coupled to the Tinguely loom
Of augmented electric music, strong
As sexuality and loud as noise,
Which keens across the dingy room at full
Gain, and, its coin gone, as abruptly dies.

IV. STAGE DOOR JOHNNY'S

Silvana Casamassima, Vic Blad
(The talent agent), Lance Bartholomey,
Piretta Paul, Max Dove, A. Lincoln Brown,
Samarra Brown, Lil Yeovil, Beryl Cohn
(Theatrical attorney), Johnny Groen
(The owner), Merritt Praed, Morty Monroe,
Dame Phyllis Woolwich, Sir Jack Handel, Bart.,
Del Specter (the producer), Coquetel,
Fab Newcomb, Temple Bell, Vanessa Vane,
Burt Wartman, C.R. Freedley, F.R.S.,
Alf Wandsworth (author of "Queer Street"), Mel Hess,
His Honor Judge Perutz, Merced McCall,
Tam Pierce, Bill Brewer, Tom Cobley, and all
The darlings, mirrored in their flourishing
Autographed caricatures on every wall,
Sail on, sealed in, important, bright, serene,
In league in Captain Nemo's submarine.

V. M. WAX LOANS

Clear and obscure, elbows of saxophones
Shine out like sink traps in an underworld
Of pledges unredeemed: a spectral band
Of brass and nickel marching in the dark
Toward the morning and redemption, where
Known lips will kiss their reeds, familiar hands
Resume their old and loving fingering.
Unlikely: in a hundred rented rooms
From here to Ybor City, pledgors plan
What next to pawn: the Rolleicord, the ring,
The eight-transistor Victor radio,

The travelling alarm. Alarm creeps in-
To all their calculations, now the bloom
Is off their promise, now the honeymoon
Is over with a cry, and time begins
To whittle expectations to a size
Convenient for their carrying to pawn.

VI.   LOVEMOVIE

Before the glazed chrome case where Lovelies Swim
Au Natural, and under the sly lights
Which wink and bump and wink and grind, except
For those that have burnt out, the singing strings
Of Madame Violin essay "Caprice,"
Not missing many notes, considering
How cold it is outside the Lovemovie.
Stray pennies in her tin cup punctuate
The music like applause. Play, gypsies! Dance!
The thin strains of a Romany romance
Undaunt the ears of each peajacketed
Seaman on liberty, and of each old
Wanderer slowly losing to the cold,
And of each schoolboy who has come to see
Life in the flesh inside the Lovemovie.
Beneath her stiff green hair, an artist's grin
Knits up the ravelled cheek of Madame Violin.

VII.   THE ARGO BUILDING:
NEW DELMAN'S GOOD NIGHT

The last bone button in the old tin tea
Box of the Argo Building lastly sees
GNIVAEWER ELBISIVNI peeling off
His street-side window as he locks the door
Of 720 one more night, and struts

His septuagenarian stuff down
The corridor, past Aabco Dental Labs,
Worldwide Investigations, Inc., Madame
Lillé, Corsetiere, Star School of Tap,
Dr. O'Keefe, Franck Woodwind Institute,
Wink Publications, and Watch Hospital.
Up the wrought shaft, preceded by its wires
Ticking and twittering, the intrepid car
Rises like an old aeronaut to take
Its ballast-passenger aboard beneath
The pointed clear bulbs of its four flambeaux,
Sweetly attenuated art nouveau
Which was *vieux jeu* and is the rage, unknown
To old New Delman, whom it ferries down
In its black cage, funebrially slow,
To Stygian Forty-Seventh Street below.

The Nanny Boat, 1957

Towards the end he sailed into an extraordinary mildness,
And anchored in his home and reached his wife
And rode within the harbour of her hand . . .
                                        — *W. H. Auden*

Relish the love of a gentle woman.
                    — *John Cheever*

I. DOWN

1.

A surf of people, backlit by the sun,
Washes across Atlantic Avenue
To Rowe's Wharf, where the Nanny Boat awaits
Its gilt-edged Friday-night commuters, borne
Out of the city on a roasting wave
Of Victor Coffee. Soon that city scent
Gives in to those of shore and sea. You step
Infinitely daintily, treading my heart
With your white size-five foot, aboard the boat
Bound for Nantasket and for night, where you
Will understudy seas in undulant
Compliance and reception, swamping all
My longboat adjectives. Cast off the bow
And stern lines linking us to the upright,
August, and sobersided city, and
Back half-speed out into the glassy reach —
Cased yellow by the molten sun — which leads
South to anonymous liberties, where town
Clothes come ungirt and naked bankers lie
Late on the sand beside associates.

2.

My Nikon neatly juxtaposes you,
Tall, dominant, with the recessive, squat
Skyline of Boston, in its unabridged
Wide-angle condensation. Click, and it
Is history, distorted, black-and-white,
And two-dimensional at that. (Think now,
Eight good years later, of those passages
To sea and not to sea, those passages
Between us which we shared with Spectacle
Island and Gallup's Island, those long green
Fluent quotations of cold fact and salt
Occurrences about the boat, which, aureous,
For the short span of sunset, blanched and went blue
When day was done.) Later, the running lights,
The dusty bulbs above the bar, the cream
Fluorescent strips refract on the night air
And make a great white, green, red, cream
Mirage on the horizon, even beyond
Hull Gut and Bumpkin Island. The Sturgeon Moon
Levers itself, yellow as piano keys,
Out of the eastern sea and stains the waves
Its summer color. Lovers, limited,
Perhaps, to this boat ride to demonstrate
Their aims, melt into one under the moon
Along the promenade deck; we, sedate,
Smoke, knowing we can well afford to wait
For spring tides in the middle of the night.

II. THERE

1.

The far mirage is an oasis now:
Beyond World's End, the spitting negative

Image of the city we left at five
Takes shape in the solutions of the sea.
Black towers go white, and, shivering to the shore,
Lead our wide eyes up white towers in the air
Above the sky signs advertising love
In a lost language: O's of ferris wheels,
The cursive of the roller coaster, scrawls
Of neon on the rooflines of dance halls,
All ciphers for a scholar to decode.
Your face, a spectrogram, reflects their shades
Of meaning, green, red, white, as we slip in
To dock at this free port of noise, whose din —
Calliopes, pop records, human cries —
Projects the same sensational offer of
Love for mere money, though the easy terms
Are unintelligible through
The language barrier, *comprenez-vous?*
But on the dock, spelled out in silver light
Dispensed by Paragon Park, we read two old
Familiar names, Frannie and Ed, who wait
In the old yellow Willys wagon. Friends,
Greet two new voyagers to the World's End.

2.

Out those wide windows Hingham paints itself,
Impeccably, if academically,
In the low-key, representational
Shades of a summer night. Well to the west,
A knot of lights, the Center, sends a line
In Morse across the water to Crow Point,
Calling my maritime interests to
Three granite islets, possibly archly named
Ragged, Sarah, Langlee, harboring

Just underneath my window. The moon's sway
As night-light laureate is threatened by
Arc lightning in the western front of cloud.
My host's voice calls me back. I wake and drown
In the dry world of letters. "Lefty, you
Don't really mean it about Gilbert, do
You, seriously, I mean?" "Why, sure I do,"
I say. "Come on, just tell me who
Else wrote a decent line of satire in
The bloody century. Why, Porter and
The Major-General are radical
Caricatures, Ed, archetypes." "Go *on!*"
"No, really." "Hell, let's have a nightcap." "Yeah!"
We toast our differences in B.P.R.
And Pierce's No. 6 commingled. Wug!
That's bracing going down. The evening ends
In inconclusion, as it should with friends.

3.

To quote my later self, "I punctuate
Your long body with exclamations." Not
Terribly temperate; nor was I then,
Between a skinful of cheap rye and a
Head full of Great Ideas. Then there was you
To blame, with that invisible smirk
I could see as plain as anything in the dark,
And your slow pulse just slipping up the shore
And barely sliding back, and worst of all,
Your cool electrifying skin humming
With wattage waiting for the switch to close.
Fused and short-circuited at last, we doze
Until a jovial thunderclap hits home
And takes our pictures with a massive flash

That just goes on and on, while we sit up
Like couples caught by eyes in hotel rooms,
And face the music. Rain comes down like doom.

III. BACK

1.

A bodkin through my head, I watch the view,
Which, as a dayscape, paints itself anew
(With cunning strokes around the shoreline), while
I wait for bacon frying. Mesmerized
By smoke from your bent Viceroy, you still sit
Cross-legged on the sofa, eyes at ease.
Soon we will fly from this well-ordered here,
Complete with friends, to an amorphous there,
Hull down on the horizon, where we will
Take steps to walk together or apart.
Whichever, in this moment I concede
Your beauty and necessity aside
From any need of mine, which makes my need
Decided and imperative. Be mine.

2.

Pink stucco steams behind us as we steam
Away from hot Nantasket, where the brass
Poles of the carousels, the steering wheels
Of dodgems, and the rusty grab rails on
The front of roller-coaster cars are all
Too hot to touch, and where the towering
Totems of Popeye, Jiggs, and Mickey Mouse
(Done by some village Lichtenstein, some mute
Inglorious Warhol using old house paint)
Peel in the August sun, while we creep in
To the tiny shade of the top deck, drinking

Warm, sticky Coke in paper cups. They pass,
The harbor islands, one by one, astern,
Rapt in a heat haze. The sleek, moneyed sea,
All gold and green, turns in its figured sheets
As it sleeps off a stormy night. We draw
The city slowly closer to our bow.

3.

All this our north stinks peace. The cabbage leaves
Downtrodden on the Market cobbles, and
The fish heads festering in garbage cans
Outside the shuttered fish stores lend their loud
Saturday odors to disturb the peace
Of Sunday in the city. Carrying
Your Winship overnight bag, I walk up
The shady side of every street beside
You, to the desert waste of Cambridge Street.
We brave the sun to cross. Around the bend
Under the El, and up West Cedar Street,
And up four flights to your apartment, where
You turn the fan on, and I'm home
At last with you the first time in my life,
My anchor, my harbor, my second wife.

Love-Making; April; Middle Age

A fresh west wind from water-colored clouds
Stirs squills and iris shoots across the grass
Now turning fiery green. This storm will pass
In dits and stipples on the windowpane
Where we lie high and dry, and the low sun
Will throw rose rays at our grey heads upon
The back-room bed's white pillows. Venus will
Descend, blue-white, in horizontal airs
Of red, orange, ochre, lemon, apple green,
Cerulean, azure, ultramarine,
Ink, navy, indigo, at last midnight.
Now, though, this clouded pewter afternoon
Blurs in our window and intensifies
The light that dusts your eyes and mine with age.

We turn our thirties over like a page.

Dying: An Introduction

Always too eager for future, we
Pick up bad habits of expectancy.
— *Philip Larkin*

I. RING AND WALK IN

Summer still plays across the street,
An ad-hoc band
In red, white, blue, and green
Old uniforms
And borrowed instruments;
Fall fills the street
From shore to shore with leaves,
A jaundiced mass
Movement against the cold;
I slip on ice
Slicks under powder snow and stamp my feet
Upon the doctor's rubber mat,
Ring and Walk In
To Dr. Sharon's waiting room,
For once with an appointment,
To nonplus
Ugly Miss Erberus.
Across from other candidates —
A blue-rinsed dam
In Davidows, a husk
Of an old man,
A one-eyed boy — I sit
And share their pervigilium.
One *Punch* and two
*Time*s later comes the call.

II. PROBABLY NOTHING

Head cocked like Art, the *Crimson* linotype
Operator, Dr. Sharon plays
Taps on my game leg, spelling out the name,
With his palpating fingers, of my pain.
The letters he types are not visible
To him or me; back up the melting pot
Of the machine, the matrix dents the hot
Lead with a letter and another: soon a word,
Tinkling and cooling, silver, will descend
To be imposed upon my record in
Black-looking ink. "My boy, I think," he says,
In the most masterly of schoolish ways,
In the most quiet of all trumps in A
Flat, "this lump is probably nothing, but"—
A but, a buzz of omen resonates —
"I'd check it anyway. Let's see when I
Can take a specimen." Quiet business
With the black phone's bright buttons. St, ssst, sst:
An inside call. In coded whispers. Over. Out.
"Can you come Friday noon? We'll do it then."
I nod I can and pass the world of men
In waiting, one *Life* farther on.

III. O.P.O.R.

Undressing in the locker room
Like any high school's, full of shades
In jockstraps and the smell of steam,
Which comes, I guess, from autoclaves,
And not from showers, I am struck
By the immutability,
The long, unchanging, childish look

Of my pale legs propped under me,
Which, nonetheless, now harbor my
Nemesis, or, conceivably,
Do not. My narcissistic eye
Is intercepted deftly by
A square nurse in a gas-green gown
And aqua mask — a dodo's beak —
Who hands me a suit to put on
In matching green, and for my feet
Two paper slippers, mantis green:
My invitation to the dance.
I shuffle to the table, where
A shining bank of instruments —
Service for twelve — awaits my flesh
To dine. Two nurses pull my pants
Down and start shaving. With a splash,
The Doctor stops his scrubbing-up
And walks in with a quiet "Hi."
Like hummingbirds, syringes tap
The novocain and sting my thigh
To sleep, and the swordplay begins.
The stainless-modern knife digs in —
Meticulous trencherman — and twangs
A tendon faintly. Coward, I groan.
Soon he says "Sutures," and explains
To me he has his specimen
And will stitch up, with boundless pains,
Each severed layer, till again
He surfaces and sews with steel
Wire. "Stainless." Look how thin it is,
Held in his forceps. "It should heal
Without a mark." These verities
Escort me to the tiring room,
Where, as I dress, the Doctor says,
"We'll have an answer Monday noon."

I leave to live out my three days,
Reprieved from findings and their pain.

IV. PATH. REPORT

Bruisingly cradled in a Harvard chair
Whose orange arms cramp my pink ones, and whose black
Back stamps my back with splat marks, I receive
The brunt of the pathology report,
Bitingly couched in critical terms of my
Tissue of fabrications, which is bad.
That Tyrian specimen on the limelit stage
Surveyed by Dr. Cyclops, magnified
Countless diameters on its thick slide,
Turns out to end in -oma. "But be glad
These things are treatable today," I'm told.
"Why, fifteen years ago —" a dark and grave-
Shaped pause. "But now, a course of radiation, and —"
Sun rays break through. "And if you want X-ray,
You've come to the right place." A history,
A half-life of the hospital. Marie
Curie must have endowed it. Cyclotrons,
Like missile silos, lurk within its walls.
It's reassuring, anyway. But bland
And middle-classic as these environs are,
And sanguine as his measured words may be,
And soft his handshake, the webbed, inky hand
Locked on the sill, and the unshaven face
Biding outside the window still appall
Me as I leave the assignation place.

V. OUTBOUND

Outside, although November by the clock,
Has a thick smell of spring,

And everything —
The low clouds lit
Fluorescent green by city lights;
The molten, hissing stream
Of white car lights, cooling
To red and vanishing;
The leaves,
Still running from last summer, chattering
Across the pocked concrete;
The wind in trees;
The ones and twos,
The twos and threes
Of college girls,
Each shining in the dark,
Each carrying
A book or books,
Each laughing to her friend
At such a night in fall;
The two-and-twos
Of boys and girls who lean
Together in an A and softly walk
Slowly from lamp to lamp,
Alternatively lit
And nighted; Autumn Street,
Astonishingly named, a rivulet
Of asphalt twisting up and back
To some spring out of sight — and everything
Recalls one fall
Twenty-one years ago, when I,
A freshman, opening
A green door just across the river,
Found the source
Of spring in that warm night,
Surprised the force
That sent me on my way

And set me down
Today. Tonight. Through my
Invisible new veil
Of finity, I see
November's world —
Low scud, slick street, three giggling girls —
As, oddly, not as sombre
As December,
But as green
As anything:
As spring.

Canzone: Aubade

Morning, noon, afternoon, evening, and night
Are not all seasons that we need to know;
Though we would go lamely without the night,
Recircling on itself, night after night,
Assuring us an opposite, a way
To action of a kind that honest night
Would never dream of, sibilant brief night
Could not conceive: the bitter stroke of noon.
Better that we conceive of dawn than noon,
That place where all things shift, and middle night
Sits for its portrait in half light, and still
Sits obstinately in two lights, quite still.

Though dawn is at the window, you, all still,
Take the small part of small hours of the night
And sleep away the morning, small and still,
Till my minuscule action wakes you. Still,
I cannot think that you, awaking, know
The whispered confidence of nighttime still.
Outside, the city's streets are silent still;
And morning still attempts to find a way
To say itself; and donkey's years away
Keeps hot important midday, trying still
To blandish us with talk of afternoon;
But we know now the pitilessness of noon.

I cannot think of you at all at noon
As my late lover whose long body still
I punctuate with exclamations. Noon —

The rigid, brazen, upright arm of noon —
Casts a long shadow between now and night
Where intervened the tortuous forenoon:
The twice-told tale of snaillike afternoon,
That we know better than we need to know.
What is there, after all, for us to know
That meaning clings to in the eye of noon?
Through the slow afternoon we seek a way
Of meeting evening's sullen change halfway.

Now it is middle afternoon, halfway
To evening; and, looking back on noon,
I marvel to have found some kind of way
To pass the stolid hours that guard you. Way
Off somewhere in the darkness you lie still,
Not quite recapturable, and part way
To capturing you my thought falls away
To urgencies of afternoon. All night
Your phosphorescence clarifies the night,
Makes light of darkness, indicates the way
To tunnels' ending: darling, you must know
The dead-white end of the dark road we know.

New schemes, new modes, new paradigms? We know
All of our love must go the same old way.
We must discredit learning; all I know
Is evening keeping us apart. You know
Like me that memory at noon
Springs on us all the secrets that we know
About ourselves, to try if we can know
The agony of aloneness. Lying still,
We paint ourselves all black. O lover, still
It stirs me every evening to know
We pay such court to turnings in the night;
And my thoughts take you as if day were night.

ENVOY

At last, alas! day is born out of night,
And, though our pain persists in sleeping still,
It will arise and flourish at high noon,
And furious, constant, seek to find a way
Out of our time, the only one we know.